Chinese Sculpture, Bronzes, and Jades in Japanese Collections

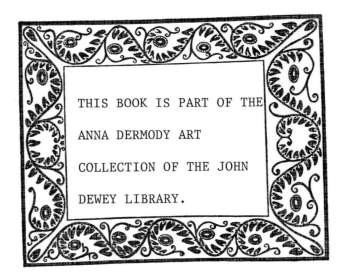

CHINESE SCULPTURE, BRONZES, AND JADES IN JAPANESE COLLECTIONS

by Yūzō Sugimura

English Adaptation by Burton Watson

East-West Center Press, Honolulu

Copyright © 1966 in Japan by Bijutsu Shuppan-sha

Published in Japan Bijutsu Shuppan-sha, Tokyo

Published outside Japan by East-West Center Press, Honolulu

Library of Congress Card Catalog Number 66-22477

Printed and bound in Japan

FOREWORD

〈

CHINESE ART, WITH a history that begins in Neolithic times and continues unbroken to the present day, embraces many genres and media of expression. Three of the most important styles are represented in this volume: the beautiful tomb figures that were made to guard and accompany the bodies of the dead; the bronze and stone sculpture of Chinese Buddhism; and the famous bronze vessels and jade carvings of the ancient period. The works represented here, all of them in public and private collections in Japan, include some of the finest examples of these genres to be found anywhere in the world. One of the leading Japanese authorities on Chinese art, Professor Yūzō Sugimura of the Tokyo National Museum, has written texts dealing with each of these genres, giving a general survey of their development and providing the information necessary to an appreciation of the background and importance of the pieces reproduced.

This is an exciting time for both scholars and laymen interested in Chinese art, and particularly in the art of the early period. Archaeological excavations conducted in China in recent decades have brought to light countless works of rare beauty and inestimable historical importance, as well as other finds of great value to the expert. Thanks to these excavations, we now know far more about the history and culture of early China than did the scholars of preceding centuries, and there is every reason to believe that further excavations and surveys will enable us to learn even more.

As a result of these rapid advances in our understanding of Chinese archaeology and art history, our picture of the early period is constantly changing. Long-established suppositions are being over-turned, dates for the earliest occurrence of particular art forms or media are being pushed back, and new theories and interpretations advanced.

Many of these important new discoveries will be described or referred to in the text. For example, the frontispiece shows a lovely little ceramic statue of a dancing girl, with long sleeves and a highly conventionalized face, that is remarkably similar in treatment to works of modern sculpture. It dates from the so-called Warring States period, which lasted from 403 to 221 B.C. Until about twenty years ago, when this dancing girl and other tomb figures like her came to light, the existence of such ceramic figures during that period was entirely unknown. Their discovery, therefore, has not only helped our understanding of the development of tomb figures in China but has also provided valuable information on the costume of the period.

Until the present time, so far as I am aware, no scholar has offered an explanation of why the face of the dancing girl is so drastically simplified in treatment, though many have remarked on it. Recently, Professor Shigeki Kaizuka of Kyoto University, in his work on Chinese mythology entitled *Kamigami no tanjo*[1] (The Birth of the Gods), offers the suggestion that the figure represents a dancing female shaman impersonating a spirit of the dead. She wears a mask, as was customary in such rituals, and the mask is almost featureless, since the ancient Chinese believed this was the appropriate way to represent the spirits of the departed. Professor Kaizuka's theory may be confirmed in time by the results of further excavation and study; or, like

[1] "Green Belt Series" (Tokyo: Chikuma Shobo, 1963).

many of the tentative and probing suggestions of scholars, it may have to be modified or discarded. This example will indicate to the reader that the history of Chinese art is anything but cut and dried at present; any statement made today may have to be altered tomorrow.

The example cited above concerns the history of Chinese tomb figures; similar examples could be given in relation to the history of bronzes or of Buddhist sculpture. Our entire concept of the history of bronze culture in China, as well as our knowledge of casting techniques and our interpretation of the art motifs of Chinese bronzes, has been changing as a result of the archaeological finds of recent years. And though the finds relating to Buddhist art have been less spectacular than those of the ancient period, our understanding of Chinese Buddhist art, and of its relationship to the Buddhist art of India and Central Asia, is progressing steadily. Needless to say, the most important contributions to our knowledge have been made by the Chinese themselves. But there is also a growing body of scholars in Japan, Europe, and the United States who, working often with the techniques of comparative archaeology and art history,

are throwing new light upon the history and development of Chinese art, as well as introducing abroad the most important researches of Chinese scholars.

The present volume, I hope, will help to acquaint the English reader with some of the important genres and individual works of art of the magnificent Chinese tradition. The plates and text have been divided into three sections dealing with tomb figures, Buddhist sculpture, and ancient bronzes and jades. In adapting Professor Sugimura's Japanese text I have taken the liberty of rearranging the order of some of the material and of adding other material that I felt would help the English reader understand the history and background of the various periods. The text covers the general history of the styles, but particular information on works reproduced here has been included in the notes to the plates. Every effort has been made to give as much information as possible about the pieces reproduced, although certain unavoidable gaps in the data remain. Where no notation on the present location of a piece is included, it is understood to be in a private collection.

BURTON WATSON

Kyoto, 1963

CONTENTS

PART I TOMB SCULPTURE

WHEN DID MAN first become convinced that, although the body dies and decays, the spirit lives on after death and must therefore be provided with food and utensils in the same way as when the body was living? Probably very early in his development. In China, from evidence found at sites of the so-called Yang-shao culture, we can date such a belief as early as the Neolithic era.

The term "Yang-shao," derived from the location of a major archaeological site in Honan, designates a culture centered in the upper Yellow River Valley, developed by proto-Chinese and characterized by pottery made of red clay and often decorated with painting. In 1954 an important site belonging to this culture was discovered on a hilltop at Pan-p'o Village in the bank of the Ch'an River, east of Sian in Shensi. Many pieces of pottery were excavated from graves at this site, including a bowl with a remarkably skillful painting of a human head topped with an elaborate headdress. This bowl, which, incidentally, bears the earliest known example in Chinese art of a painting of the human face, may well have been made for daily use. But the fact that it was buried with the dead shows that the concept of funerary offerings and furniture was already in existence.

A second culture, roughly contemporary with the Yang-shao, appeared to the east, around Shantung, on the great flood plains of the Yellow River. This is characterized by unpainted pottery made of black clay and, from the name of its principal site, is known as the Lung-shan culture. These two cultures were eventually replaced in the central area of China by a third culture, characterized by gray pottery shaped with a pad and beater.

While these developments were taking place, the Neolithic villages, often quite densely distributed throughout the plains and surrounded by thick walls of tamped earth, were growing in size. Local leaders appeared, who gained control of a number of these villages and combined their populations, forming towns and cities. Finally, around the eighteenth century B.C., a dynasty of kings known as the Shang, or Yin, rose to power in the area around the central part of the Yellow River.

Ancient Chinese literature preserves a number of accounts of the Shang Dynasty, but until the present century there was no reliable archaeological evidence of its existence. At the end of the nineteenth century, however, certain scholars noticed the peculiar writing on some "dragon bones"— old bones sold at pharmacies to be ground to a powder and used in making medicine. Eventually it was realized that these were bones used in an ancient type of divination. Their origin was traced to a village near An-yang in Honan, which, on excavation, proved to have been the site of the main capital of the Shang Dynasty. The capital was probably founded in the thirteenth century B.C., and was occupied until the dynasty's downfall in 1027 B.C., (according to the chronology of the *Bamboo Annals*). Since 1928 thorough excavations have been carried out at this site, and in recent years more than seventy additional Shang sites have been excavated, some of them predating the An-yang site.

Among the many important finds made at An-yang, the most pertinent to our discussion are the magnificent tombs of the Shang rulers. The largest of these measures 43 feet deep and 55 feet square. The tombs are often in the form of a cross, with stairways at each side, a ramp on the south, and a wooden coffin chamber sunk in the center. After interment had taken place, the entire excavation was filled with tamped earth.

Frequently found interred with the Shang rulers were human attendants—men, women, and even

1

babies—sometimes decapitated, their heads, and bodies buried separately; sometimes they were kneeling as guardians, armed and attended by dogs. A study of their skeletons reveals that the majority were young when they chose—or were forced—to "follow in death" (*hsün-ssu*), as the Chinese term puts it, their rulers. Some may have been ladies in waiting or favored ministers of the dead ruler; but most were slaves, perhaps prisoners captured in the Shang's wars with neighboring peoples.

In addition to these human attendants, the Shang kings and queens were buried with many of the articles they had loved and used in life: carved jade ornaments; clothes boxes inlaid with precious stones, shell, or ivory (from which the clothes themselves, through decay, had long since disappeared); bows, arrows, spears, and other weapons; and bronze sacrificial vessels. In the larger tombs, whole carriages were interred, along with the horses that drew them, as well as sheep, cattle, deer, and elephants.

Early Chinese works often speak of the extreme piety and attention to the service of the spirits that characterized the Shang people.[2] Most of what we know of Shang history and society is based upon information found in the inscriptions on the bones and tortoise shells which they used for divination, for the Shang rulers were careful to consult the spirits of their ancestors before making decisions. Sacrifices to these spirits and to nature deities played an important role in their lives, as did the diviners and shamans who acted as mouthpieces of the supernatural. Apparently, the Shang people believed in a life after death, where the departed rulers would use the articles buried with them; would be attended by the people and animals who had followed them in death, be fed by the sacrifices of their descendants, and, perhaps, be rejuvenated by the souls of the little children sacrificed at their interment. For all we know, death may not have been to these people the fearful event it is to modern man, and many of the followers of the ruler, caught up in the intense religious excitement of a royal

burial, may have gone willingly and without regret to join their lord in his new life.

The Shang state, probably no more than a loose confederation of clans acknowledging the sovereignty of the Shang king, was eventually conquered by a vigorous new clan known as the Chou, who spread east of their home in the Wei River Valley in Shensi. In various strategic areas of eastern and central China, the Chou leaders enfeoffed the members of their families and their principal followers and allies, as well as the descendants of the Shang royal line. The leaders, however, returned to their old home in western China and built their main capital at a site west of present-day Sian. Early Chou-period sites have recently been uncovered in this area, including tombs containing dogs, horses, carriages, and a few human "followers of the dead," which suggests that early Chou burial customs resembled those of Shang times. So far, however, no remains of the Chou capital have come to light.

The Chou royal house, after an initial period of vigor and widespread conquest, did not fare well in its western capital, and in 770 B.C., was forced by foreign invaders to flee east and take up residence in the city of Lo, its eastern capital, near present-day Lo-yang. This event divides the chronology of the Chou Dynasty into two periods: the Western Chou (1027?–771 B.C.) and the Eastern Chou (770–249 B.C.). After its move to the east, the Chou Dynasty was seldom able to command more than nominal allegiance from its vassals. Its own power dwindled, while that of the more important feudal princes, such as the rulers of the state of Chin in the north, Ch'i on the Shantung Peninsula, and Ch'u and Wu in the lower Yangtze Valley, continued to grow.

The custom of human sacrifice on the death of a ruler continued sporadically in the early part of this period. The most notorious example occurred in 621 B.C., when, according to the *Tso Chuan* (Tso's Commentary on the *Spring and Autumn Annals*) (Duke Wen 5th Year), three high ministers of the state of Ch'in were put to death to accompany their deceased ruler, Duke Mu. The *Shih Chi*,

2 E. g. *Shih Chi* (Records of the Historian), chap. 8.

(Records of the Historian), a somewhat later source, gives 170 as the number of men sacrificed on this occasion. The event is particularly famous because the *Book of Odes*[3] records a song said to have been composed by the grief-stricken people of the state, the first stanza of which reads:

> *Yellow birds dart and turn,*
> *Perch in the thorn tree.*
> *Who follows Duke Mu?*
> *Yen-hsi of Tzu-chü clan.*
> *This Yen-hsi,*
> *Worth a hundred men,*
> *At the brink of the pit*
> *Trembles and shakes with fear.*
> *Blue Heaven above,*
> *You slay our good men!*
> *Could we but ransom him*
> *A hundred men were cheap!*

The state of the Ch'in, which occupied the old capital area of Western Chou, was regarded by the more highly civilized states of the east as semi-barbaric, and the above incident was often cited as evidence of its barbaric ways. The custom of human sacrifice had apparently died out in the east, or was rapidly falling into disrepute. A reminder of it remained, however, in the form of the *mu-yung*, or wooden dolls, that were buried with the dead.

We find an early mention of these dolls, or tomb figures, in the *Tso Chuan*, in an entry dated 539 B.C. (Duke Chao 3rd year). In an anecdote related in this passage (which may be of later date), Duke Ching of Ch'i is pictured urging his high minister Yen Ying to move from his old home near the city market to a quieter and more pleasant location. Yen Ying, however, declines, saying that he prefers his present house. The duke remarks that since he lives so close to the market he must know the price of goods, and asks which goods are expensive and which cheap. Duke Ching at this time was noted for the severity of his rule and the large number of men he condemned to punishment, and Yen Ying seizes the opportunity to deliver an indirect

reprimand. "Tomb dolls (*yung*) are expensive," he replies, "but shoes are cheap!"

In the *Book of Ritual*,[4] Confucius is recorded as speaking of tomb articles in these words: "He who makes 'spirit articles' [*ming ch'i*, articles especially for the dead] understands the proper way of burial. Even though one has a supply of real articles, they must not be used—it would be too pitiful for the dead to use articles that belong to the living. It would be hardly different from using human sacrifices, would it? The so-called spirit articles belong to the spirits—clay carts and figures made of straw —they have been used since ancient times. They are the proper spirit articles. . . . Those who make figures of straw are good men, but those who make dolls are lacking in benevolence. Making such dolls is hardly different from using real men, is it?"

This chapter in the *Book of Ritual* appears to be a genuine text of late Chou times, and though it may not reflect Confucius' own views, it certainly does those of the followers of the Confucian school at that time. Again, in the writings of Hsün Tzu, a Confucian philosopher of the third century B.C., we find the same point made: that articles intended for the use of the dead must be different from those used by the living.[5] The Confucians apparently felt that the wooden dolls in use at this time were too realistic, and might lead men to go a step farther and substitute real human sacrifices for the harmless dolls. This is the background of the famous statement in *Mencius*:[6] "Chung-ni [Confucius] said, 'Because he made images of men and used them, the man who first invented tomb dolls must surely have died without heirs'." Again, we cannot say whether this represents the opinion of Confucius himself, although we know from the *Analects* that Confucius was very reluctant to discuss matters pertaining to death or the spirits. Apparently, the Confucians felt keenly that there was a real danger that the old custom of human sacrifice might be revived if men did not learn to distinguish once and for all between the needs of

---

[3] "Airs of Ch'in."

[4] T'an Kung Chapter, part 2.
[5] *Hsün Tzu* XIX, "A Discussion of Rites."
[6] *Book of Mencius*, IA. 4.

the living and of the dead. Hence they advocated that the wooden dolls be done away with and that men return to what they claimed was the practice of antiquity, the use of cruder figures of straw.

The actual dolls themselves, because they were made of wood, for the most part perished long ago, especially those from the early period. Recent excavations, however, have revealed examples of dolls from a slightly later time, the so-called Warring States period of the late Chou Dynasty, which lasted from 403 B.C. until the unification of China under the First Emperor of Ch'in in 221 B.C. These came from two sites, Ch'ang-sha in Hunan and Hsin-yang in Honan; they were preserved because of the extraordinary thickness and durability of the coffins in which they had been placed.

Excavations at the Ch'ang-sha site, which has yielded numerous articles of the Warring States and Han periods, were begun in 1931, and are still continuing. Among the finds so far reported are a painting of a woman on silk—the oldest known Chinese silk painting—writing brushes and scrapers, inscribed wooden writing tablets, toilet boxes, wooden lutes and models of boats, lacquer wine cups, ornaments of precious stones and glass, furniture, and so on. The Hsin-yang site, discovered in 1956, has yielded tomb dolls, writing tablets, musical instruments, wine cups, dishes, and numerous other wooden, lacquer, and bamboo articles. Both represent the culture of the state of Ch'u, the powerful state centered in the lower Yangtze Valley which became part of the unified empire under the Ch'in and Han dynasties.

Special attention should be called to two painted wooden statues of fabulous beasts recovered from these sites, which represent the finest examples we have of Chou-period wooden sculptures. These figures were no doubt intended to guard the graves and drive away evil spirits, serving the same purpose as figures of the Deva Kings, or *Vajrapani*, in Buddhist art. The creatures represent a being known as a *t'ao-t'ieh*. The *t'ao-t'ieh* motif is very common in the bronze and jade decorations of the Shang and early Chou periods, and will be discussed in greater detail in Part III. By late Chou times, it

should be noted, this fabulous monster had become a symbol of gluttony, and its insatiable appetite, therefore, made it an appropriate guardian against evil spirits. In these particular representations, the *t'ao-t'ieh's* proverbial appetite is symbolized by its long, protruding tongue, a feature not characteristic of earlier representations. It is interesting to speculate whether this feature had some influence upon later stone representations of lions —also marked by protruding tongues—such as those which were set up in the sixth century to guard the tombs of the rulers of the southern dynasties near Nanking.

In addition to these wooden tomb figures, others made of clay, which date from the Warring States period, have been found in the Yellow River region. A group of these, made of black pottery and measuring about 4 inches high were found in the district of Hui in Honan. After having been fired to produce a jet-black color, the surfaces were polished to a fine luster, and red pigment was then applied to the faces and other parts. Dancing girls, warriors, horses, wine bowls, and mirrors are among objects represented. The dancing girls, with their large faces, narrow conventionalized noses, and graceful sleeves, are among the most skillfully executed. Plates 1 and 2 represent figures from this set.

These figures came to light around 1942, at the height of the war, and the place and circumstances of their discovery are a matter of doubt. Designs on the bowls and mirrors in the group, as well as other features of the pieces, tally exactly with the style of works unquestionably of the Warring States period, and it is quite clear that they are not calculated fakes. But the number of pieces in the group is small, and almost all of them were brought to Japan from Peking. Later, models of some of the pieces began to circulate, and as a result scholars in America, China, and elsewhere have on occasion questioned the authenticity of the entire group. In 1955, however, at a site near the city of Ch'ang-chin in Shansi, a very similar group of figures was found. Though not executed with such skill as those in the group found earlier, they clearly belong to the same type, and since Ch'ang-chin is no great distance from the alleged site of the earlier discovery, there seems no reason to doubt that the earlier figures were actually found in the district of Hui, which was the site of a major city of the state of Wei during the Warring States period.

The Han Dynasty, which replaced the short-lived Ch'in in 202 B.C., and ruled, with the exception of a short break in the middle, until A.D. 220, reached artistic heights second only to those of the ancient Shang. Under the strong-willed Emperor Wu (140–87 B.C.), the borders of the empire were extended into Central Asia on the west, the Korean Peninsula in the northeast, and Annam in the south, bringing the Chinese into direct contact with numerous foreign peoples and cultures. The extensive literature of the past was collected and edited in imperial libraries, writing was simplified, paper invented, and learning encouraged through the establishment of a government university. Iron goods, lacquer ware, and dyed cloth attained a much wider distribution among the population as a whole than ever before.

The rulers and aristocrats of this period built numerous magnificent palaces and residences; their tombs were constructed on a matching scale and were supplied, according to sources of the period, with numerous treasures and spirit articles. But, perhaps because of widespread looting of the graves (said to have been one of the most lucrative occupations of the time), or perhaps because the spirit articles were made of wood, almost none have been recovered that date from the early years of the Han.

In time, however, wooden grave objects gave place to those made of clay; these have been found in abundance, providing us with a most valuable source of information on the customs, dress, and daily life of the period. The earlier tomb figures of clay were baked, with the arms made separately and attached later. On completion, the whole figure was fitted with a suit of clothes in the manner of modern dolls. Still later, representations of clothed figures, both men and women, were produced, made all in one piece and marked by extreme simplicity of design. Paint was sometimes added,

and in some instances the pieces were glazed, the process of glazing having been known in China at least since Shang times.

A little may be said here about the particular types of persons represented by these tomb figures. Rarely does one find what appear to be members of the aristocracy, such as the stately ladies pictured in Plates 3 and 4. Instead, farmers and peasant women, or domestic servants (such as the plainly attired waiting-woman shown in Plate 5 or the animated cook, complete with chopping board, in Plate 7) may be seen, for these presumably would be of more service to the dead man than would highborn ladies and gentlemen. Superstition flourished during the Han Dynasty, and professional exorcists and geomancers were frequently called upon to drive away evil spirits and to determine lucky sites and directions. It is therefore not surprising that we find geomancers depicted among the tomb figures, such as the one seen in Plate 6, who could provide the dead with expert advice. Nor was the entertainment of the dead forgotten—many of the tomb figures represent dancing girls, magicians, and acrobats. The historian Ssu-ma Ch'ien, writing about 100 B.C., mentions the arrival at the Chinese court of entertainers from the lands of Central Asia during the reign of Emperor Wu, and states, "After the skills of the foreign magicians and tricksters had been imported into China, the wrestling matches and other displays of unusual feats developed and improved with each year, and from this time on entertainments of this type became increasingly popular."[7] Tomb figures of pole climbers, sword dancers, jugglers, tumblers, and similar entertainers have been found in large numbers, some of which may be seen in Plates 14 and 15.

In addition to human figures, models of such common household objects as drinking and eating vessels, kitchens, stoves, mortars, wells, animal pens, and fish ponds are numerous in this period. Model houses have been found, giving invaluable clues to the architecture of the time, and model

[7] *Shih Chi*, 123.

5

granaries that still contain bits of actual grain, providing equally valuable data for the study of the foodstuffs of two thousand years ago. In Plates 12 and 13 we see examples of wells and duck ponds.

Models of domestic animals, such as dogs, sheep, swine, chickens, ducks, oxen, and horses, also abound (Plates 8–13). The pig, which had been raised in China from Neolithic times, constituted a particularly important part of the diet of the upper classes, and was appropriately honored in the rituals of the nation; a whole roasted pig, along with an ox and a sheep, constituted the so-called *t'ai-lao* sacrifice traditionally offered by the emperor to Heaven and Earth, his ancestors, and later to Confucius. Examples of pigs may be seen in Plate 8. The dogs represented are of two varieties: plump house dogs, complete with collars, such as were kept to protect the home from thieves, and slimmer dogs used for hunting. An example of the former is depicted in Plate 11. The figures of oxen are often fitted with carts like those which served as the common means of transportation for the poorer people of the Han Empire. Occasionally, wild beasts, such as the rhinoceros, are also depicted. The rhinoceros, a rather rare and exotic creature to the early Chinese, is frequently mentioned in pre-Han and Han literature. Armor made of rhinoceros hide was used in late Chou times—the *Hsün Tzu* (XV), states that "men of the Ch'u make armor out of sharkskin and rhinoceros hide"—and it probably became more common in the Han era, as well as drinking utensils made of rhinoceros horn. A Han rhinoceros is seen in Plate 13, lower section. As in the case of human figures, a few of the pieces in this latter category of household objects and animals are glazed.

Horses played an important role in Han life. They were vital to the defense of the nation in its struggle with the nomadic tribes to the north and west, and were a mark of the aristocracy, who rode proudly about in their horse-drawn carriages while the commoners traveled by oxcart. The Han government was chronically short of horses and took various measures to encourage their increase and improve the breeds. Emperor Wu fought a war in Ferghana to obtain good specimens, and wrote poems of praise when a particularly fine animal came into his hands. For the feeding of his foreign mounts he had alfalfa, their favorite food, imported from Central Asia and extensively cultivated on government lands.

It is not surprising, therefore, that numerous tomb figures of these sturdy, beautifully shaped Han horses have been found. Because of their size, the horse figurines were usually made in three sections—head, body and legs—which were then fitted together; thus many of the figures found consist of only the head section, or the head and body sections. The largest complete figure that has come to light so far is that of a horse and carriage taken from a grave in Ch'eng-tu in Szechwan. The horse is 40 inches high, the carriage 33 inches, and the whole group is over 5 feet 8 inches long. In Plates 9 and 10 we see the simplest type of Han horse figure, while Plate 26, a figure of a neighing horse from the Latter Han Period, preserved in Japan, shows the magnificent build of the Han thoroughbred.

The Former or Western Han (202 B.C.–A.D. 8) made its capital at Ch'ang-an, near present-day Sian, and the Latter or Eastern Han (A.D. 25–220) at Lo-yang. Han grave mounds are still to be seen dotting the landscape around these cities, and many Han relics have been recovered from the region. The majority are of a plain gray pottery, though, as has been mentioned, a few are painted or fired with a green or brown glaze. The green glaze, through chemical change, has produced a beautiful silver sheen that is especially prized today. Wooden tomb figures have been recovered from Han-period graves at Pyongyang in Korea and Ch'ang-sha, but so far none have been found in the region of the Han capital. The pottery figures recovered from Han sites in the areas south of the Yangtze, while executed with the same simplicity as those of the north, are frequently marked by a kind of clumsy realism that makes them of less artistic interest than those of the north. This same tendency can be seen in the works of this region produced later, during the Eastern Chin and southern dynasties of the Six Dynasties period.

With the breakup of the Han Empire in A.D. 220, China entered upon an era of political chaos and disunity known as the Six Dynasties period, that lasted, almost without respite, for the next three and a half centuries, until its reunification under the Sui Dynasty in 589. Though the empire was unified for a brief period under the Western Chin (265-316), civil strife and the rising power of non-Chinese immigrant groups in the north forced the Chin court to flee south in 317 and establish a new capital at Chien-k'ang, present-day Nanking. During the following centuries, the south was ruled by a succession of weak and short-lived Chinese dynasties, while the north was controlled throughout most of the period by various Hunnish, Tibetan, Mongol, and Turkic groups. This was a time of great cultural change, particularly in the north, as the foreign social groups were gradually Sinicized and their customs assimilated into traditional Chinese ways of life. Buddhism, bringing with it new philosophical concepts and art forms, spread gradually through the society, and there was a revival of interest in Taoism and other earlier philosophies native to China.

More will be said about the art of this period in the section dealing with Buddhist sculpture. Here it is sufficient to note the effect of these social and ethnic changes upon the tomb figures of the time. One force that brought about the dissolution of the Han Empire was the growth of the powerful and independent aristocratic families in the provinces, and their seemingly unbreakable power contributed to the long-lasting political instability of the period that followed. Aristocratic ways of life and thought are reflected in the literature and art of the period, as we may see by observing the tomb figures, most of which come from the north. Figures of attendants abound, private soldiers of the great aristocrats, clad in military dress (Plates 18 and 19); in place of the simple peasant women of the Han period we find tall, slim beauties in elegant robes and marked by an air of refinement (Plates 16 and 17)—the same graceful ladies who appear in the Buddhist murals and cave sculptures of the period as attendants and donors.

An extensive trade with Central Asia and the West had been carried on from Han times, and was especially important to the states established during this period in northwestern China, through which the main trade route passed. Camel caravans passed back and forth over the Silk Road, and merchants from Central Asia spread into China and settled in its main cities, bringing with them the Buddhist religion and other elements of their native cultures. Their presence is reflected in the tomb figures of camels and foreign riders, such as are pictured in Plates 22-24. New types of music and musical instruments were also adopted from the West, and the important role music played in the lives of the people is evidenced by the figures of musicians like those in Plate 21. The horse figures of this period, compared with those of the Han period, are characterized by delicate heads and feet, and tend to be somewhat smaller. Examples are seen in Plates 20, 25 (lower section), and 27. Relatively few representations of everyday household objects have been found. It is difficult to say whether this is a reflection of the aristocratic tastes of the period, or of the prevalence of Buddhism, which promised a better life in a world hereafter, where mundane objects like mortars and kitchen stoves would not be needed. More thorough and scientific excavation of grave sites in the future may give us the answer.

Most of the tomb figures of the north are made of plain pottery painted with red, green, yellow, or white pigment. The green glaze that had been applied occasionally to pieces of the Han period is no longer used, but in the south a new type of celadon glaze was developed. Pieces with this type of glaze have been found in the area of Hangchow, dating from the time of the Eastern Chin and the later southern dynasties. This region was the site of the kingdom of Yüeh in ancient times, and such pieces are therefore known as *Yüeh-chou-yao* or *Yüeh-chou* ware. This glaze was often used on bowls, plates, and similar articles, such as the cinerary urn pictured in Plate 28, which is of somewhat later date. Tomb figures decorated with a blue-green glaze and belonging to the Three Kingdoms period (220-

7

265) have been found at Wu-ch'ang on the Yangtze, and a few other glazed pieces are known, but most of the southern figures are of plain pottery (Plate 29), crude in execution and mainly interesting for the light they shed upon the costumes and hair styles of the women of the period.

China's long period of disunion was finally brought to an end when the ruler of a new dynasty in the north, the Sui (581–618), captured Nanking in 589 and unified north and south under a single rule. The dynasty established its capital at Ch'ang-an, with an eastern capital at Lo-yang, and, though it fell after only thirty-eight years of rule, it undertook numerous public works, such as the opening of the Grand Canal to connect north and south, the building of palaces, and the repairing of the Great Wall. Arts and crafts likewise flourished during this period.

A number of extant tomb figures are commonly attributed to the Sui. The majority of these are finished with a yellowish-white glaze, though others are glazed in brown or white, or painted. In style they stand between the characteristic works of the earlier Northern Wei period (386–534), and those of the T'ang Dynasty that followed, being neither as small as the former nor as large as the latter. Examples are pictured in Plates 30 and 31.

The T'ang Dynasty, which replaced the Sui in 618, achieved new heights of cultural splendor. Profiting from the public works and centralized administration it inherited from the Sui, the new dynasty set out to expand Chinese power to the east, south, and west, much as the Han had done some seven centuries earlier under Emperor Wu. The energy which had for so long been dissipated in internal strife was now directed to the building and extension of a powerful empire. Whatever grief this process may have inflicted upon China's neighbors, it brought to the Chinese, at least to those of the upper classes, a life of unprecedented security, ease, and luxury. Though the T'ang Dynasty's military might in time faltered, and it fell prey to rebellion and disorder, it managed to survive until 906, and constituted one of the greatest ages of Chinese culture. Its poetry is con-

sidered the finest ever produced in the Chinese language, and its sculpture and other plastic arts were justly famous.

The splendor of the age is well reflected in the variety, craftsmanship, and beauty of its tomb figures. The T'ang legal code, compiled during the reign of Emperor Hsüan Tsung (713–756), decreed that officials of the third grade and above might have ninety tomb figures, those of the fifth grade and above, sixty figures; and those of the ninth grade and above, forty figures. It also fixed the height of the various types of figures. The obvious reason for such regulations is that the aristocrats and wealthy families were going to dangerous lengths in the extravagance of their burials, but, though sumptuary laws of this type were repeatedly promulgated, they seem to have had little effect. It is due primarily to the lavish burial customs of the T'ang gentry that so many specimens of these beautiful tomb figures have been recovered and may be enjoyed by art lovers of the present.

Women played an important role in T'ang court life, as two of the most famous personalities of the time—the notorious Empress Wu and the beautiful courtesan Yang Kuei-fei—attest. It is not surprising, therefore, that so many of the tomb figures are of lovely women, court ladies, dancing girls, or slim young maidens. Following the dictates of T'ang fashion, many of them wear ornaments of gold, and their heads are topped by elaborate coiffures such as that seen in Plate 38. Their faces are powdered, their cheeks and lips rouged, and flower patterns and other beauty marks adorn their faces. So extreme, in fact, were the feminine fashions of the time that one man, the poet Po Chü-i (772–846), was moved to compose a poem entitled "The Make-up Today," in which he satirized its more bizarre and outlandish forms. (See Frontispiece and Plates 38–43.)

Embassies from foreign courts poured into the T'ang capitals at Ch'ang-an and Lo-yang, and there were large settlements of foreigners in the principal cities, as well as streams of merchants with their camel caravans from Central Asia passing through. Many men of "barbarian" origin

—Syrians, Arabs, Persians, Tartars, Tibetans, Tonkinese, Koreans, and Japanese—visited the capital to study, teach, or play other important roles in the life of the nation, and Central Asian fashions in dress and custom were enthusiastically adopted by the Chinese. The cosmopolitan atmosphere of the capital is reflected in the poetry of the period, such as these lines written by the famous poet Li Po (701–762) when he was seeing a friend off to the east:

Where shall we hold our farewell?
By the Green Silk Gate of Ch'ang-an.
Barbarian girls wave their white hands
And call us in to drink from a golden jar.

Foreigners and foreign dress are often depicted in the tomb figures (Plates 22, 30, 32, 33, 36, and 37), as well as the camels which were the indispensable vehicle of the western trade (Plates 22, 34, and 44, lower section). The games and amusements that enlivened the existence of the T'ang aristocracy are also reflected in numerous tomb figures, such as those of the polo-playing men and women (Plate 30), the aristocratic ladies with their pet birds or dogs (Plates 36–39), the musicians and dancers who entertained at the houses (Plates 42 and 43), or the dwarfs who clowned for the amusement of their patrons (Plate 44, upper section). Domestic animals are also depicted, as well as household utensils and furniture such as candlestands, incense burners, ink slabs, and drinking vessels.

A special class of tomb figures, dating back to the grotesque *t'ao-t'ieh* monsters of Warring States times, are represented in the tomb guardians. These are of two types, warrior guardians and fabulous beasts. Buddhist art customarily employs figures of specific deities, such as Virupaksha, Indra, Brahma, Vaisravana, and the Deva Kings, as guardians of temples and altars. But these T'ang warrior guardians of the graves, though they resemble the figures of Buddhist iconography, are not to be identified with any particular deity. Examples may be seen in Plates 45 and 46.

In the popular religion of T'ang times, Buddhism and Taoism were inextricably mingled.

Both Buddhist and Taoist priests officiated at funerals, and the mixture of elements from the two religions is reflected in the second category of grave guardians, the fabulous and often partly human guardian beasts (Plate 47). The wings which frequently adorn them, on the other hand, probably represent Persian influence. Many are of a kind called *ch'i-t'ou*, or "devil-head" figures, grotesque creatures designed to frighten away evil influences. There was no set form for such pieces, and the artist was apparently free to use his imagination in giving expression to the desired aspects of ferocity and supernatural power. A particularly fine example, which employs flame-shaped decorations to heighten dramatic effect, may be seen in Plate 48.

Many of the T'ang tomb figures are decorated with the famous "three-color" glaze of white, yellow, and green, to which brown or indigo is sometimes added (see Colorplate 1), the bright colors running together and flowing over the figure with a beautiful luster. The unglazed figures, too, are often brightly painted with gold and other colors, as may be seen from the figure in the Frontispiece. The three-color glazed figures seem to have been manufactured principally in the area of the capitals, Ch'ang-an and Lo-yang, and are seldom found in other regions. The technique itself, however, was known elsewhere, as in the state of Pohai in eastern Manchuria, and was transmitted to Japan (though no three-color tomb figures have been found in Japan). In later times, the Khitan kingdom of Liao, which replaced Pohai, produced crude plates, dishes, and other utensils finished with the three-color glaze, but did not use it for human figures. Figures finished with this glaze, which date from Sung and Yüan times, have been found recently, but although they are of interest to the student of ceramics, they cannot match the brilliance and artistic excellence of the T'ang pieces. Some scholars believe that the T'ang three-color pieces exercised a direct influence upon similar three-color ceramics of Persia, but confirmation of this theory will have to await further archaeological excavation in Iran.

9

Part One: Commentaries on the Plates

COLORPLATES

Frontispiece. Dancing girl with high coiffure. Painted, T'ang Dynasty, height 15 inches. A figure of unparalleled excellence, representing the T'ang dancing girl in her most gorgeous attire. The costume suggests that she is dressed to perform the famous Dance of the Rainbow Skirt and the Feather Coat, mentioned by the poet Po Chü-i (A.D. 772–846) in his "Song of Unending Regret." She holds wooden instruments resembling castanets.

1 Lion. Glazed, T'ang Dynasty, height 10 7/8 inches. Lion figures are known in China from Han times on, although those in the early period more closely resemble tigers. With the introduction of Buddhism, lions were used from the Six Dynasties on as guardians of gates or Buddha figures; the larger ones were made of stone and the smaller ones of gilded bronze.

2 Spirit warrior. Three-color glaze, T'ang Dynasty, height 3 feet 3 inches. The face is painted red and the body glazed in brown, green, and white. The artists used no indigo on such figures, as they knew from experience that this color was too tranquil for the mood they were seeking to create.

3 A foreigner. Six Dynasties period, height 15 5/8 inches. The introduction of cultural elements from countries lying to the west of China—particularly that of Buddhist philosophy—greatly altered the customs, beliefs, and art styles of China during the third, fourth, and fifth centuries. Figures produced during this period, the so-called Six Dynasties period, are slim and elegant and often dressed in clothing of foreign design.

BLACK-AND-WHITE PLATES

1 Dancer. Black pottery, Warring States period (?), height 2 7/8 inches.

2 Horse and groom. Black pottery, Warring States period.

3 Figure of a woman (?). Black pottery, painted, Han Dynasty, height 9 7/8 inches.

4 Figure of a woman with long skirt. Painted, Han Dynasty, height 11 7/8 inches. During the Han period, the Chinese still sat on mats spread on the floor, so that women of the aristocracy wore very long skirts, as shown in this figure.

5 Figure of a waiting-woman. Unpainted, Han Dynasty, height 20 5/8 inches.

6 Figure of a geomancer. Unpainted, Han Dynasty, height 11 7/8 inches.

7 Cook. Green glaze, Han Dynasty, height 10 7/8 inches. Tenri Museum, Tenri.

8 Pigs. Han Dynasty. The upper figure, which looks more like a wild boar than a pig, is finished with green glaze and is 4 1/4 inches in height; the lower one is unpainted and is 9 7/8 inches long.

9 Horse. Unpainted, Han Dynasty, height 9 3/4 inches. Though this is said to be a Han piece, the rather soft, gentle modeling suggests that perhaps it belongs to the succeeding Three Kingdoms or Chin period. It is a rare example of a complete horse from the early period.

10 Horse's head. Han Dynasty, height 9 3/4 inches.

11 Barking dog. Green glaze, Han Dynasty, height 12 7/8 inches. Fujii Yurinkan, Kyoto.

12 (above) Owls. Han Dynasty, height 7 1/8 inches. Bronze vessels were often made in the form of owls, guardians of the night, and these are stone imitations of such vessels. The heads form the lids of the vessels, which were used for sacrificial wine. These pieces are particularly unusual because they are glazed in two colors, a clear brown for the body and green for the wings. Fujii Yurinkan, Kyoto.

(below) Wells of many types are depicted in Han tomb figures; some are equipped with pulleys for the well rope, some with sweeps, though the former type is more common. The sides of the well are covered with bas-reliefs of animals and human figures. Collection of Far Eastern Art, Waseda University.

13 (*above*) Duck pond. Finished in green glaze, Han Dynasty, diameter 11 7/8 inches.
(*below*) Rhinoceros. Painted, Han Dynasty, height 5 1/8 inches.

14 Acrobat. Painted, Han Dynasty.

15 Acrobats. Painted, Han Dynasty. The figures above are 2 5/8 to 3 1/8 inches in height. The figure on the right below balances a long pole on his shoulders, atop which another acrobat will perform stunts. That on the left below, perhaps a clown, looks up with an expression of mock astonishment and fear.

16 Waiting woman with silk head cover. Painted, Six Dynasties, height 23 inches. This lovely figure is marked by the tall stature and fine posture typical of a woman of the north. The silk head cover, worn by members of the court at this time, completely covers her high coiffure. Collection Hosokawa Goryu.

17 Man with raised finger. Painted, Six Dynasties, height 20 3/4 inches. The long skirt suggests an informal type of dress worn at home, while the narrow sleeves indicate that this is a "barbarian" or foreign-style costume.

18 Man is battle dress. Painted, Six Dynasties, height 16 1/8 inches. The figure probably held a sword and shield in its hands, though these are now missing. It wears armor of thick cloth or leather fastened with cords.

19 Man in battle dress. Painted, Six Dynasties, height 15 3/4 inches. The figure wears armor plated with iron, and originally held a spear. The helmet is made of bronze or iron. The trousers are of leather, the lines indicating the seams.

20 Musician on horseback. Painted, Six Dynasties, height 10 3/4 inches. The horse is typical of this period, with small head and powerful body.

21 Musicians playing hand drum and flute. Six Dynasties, height 11 3/8 inches (left figure) and 10 7/8 inches (right figure). From early times on, many different musical instruments were imported to China from Central Asia, which seems to have been particularly fertile in musical development. The T'o-pa Turks who ruled the north during the Northern Wei period (A.D. 386-554) were particularly active in the introduction of new instruments and musical forms.

22 Camel and barbarian rider. Painted, T'ang Dynasty, height 29 1/4 inches.

23 Camel and barbarian rider. Painted, Six Dynasties, height 10 5/8 inches. An example of a typical Central Asian merchant customarily described by the Chinese as "red-haired and green-eyed."

24 Camel. Painted, Six Dynasties. In winter the camel's hair grows long, as shown in this figure. The pack on its back is probably embroidered in the bright patterns popular among the people of Central Asia. A hare hangs from the pack.

25 (*above*) Dog. Painted, Six Dynasties, height 8 inches. This is a hunting dog, the so-called "Western Dog," bred in Central Asia and much prized in China. Dogs of this same breed are found in the area today.
(*below*) Horse. Painted, Six Dynasties, height 8 inches.

26 Neighing horse. Painted; Latter Han Dynasty; height 32 inches, length 41 inches. This is one of the largest Chinese horses to be found in Japanese collections. Han horses of similar size have recently come to light in Szechwan.

27 Horse biting its foot. Plain pottery with white paint, Six Dynasties, height 15 inches. Collection Hosokawa Goryu.

28 Cinerary urn decorated with figures of musicians. Yüeh-chou Ware, T'ang Dynasty.

29 Old man with stooped shoulders. Thin yellow glaze, early T'ang Dynasty. This piece, which dates from the end of the Sui or from the early T'ang, probably depicts an old porter.

30 Woman in foreign dress riding a horse. Yellow glaze, painted, T'ang Dynasty, height 16 3/8 inches.

31 Woman on horseback wearing a hat. Yellow-white glaze, painted, Sui Dynasty, height 13 7/8 inches.

32 Barbarian. T'ang Dynasty, height 15 3/4 inches. The prominent nose marks the man immediately as one of Turkish or Iranian blood.

33 Barbarian with a pack. T'ang Dynasty.

34 Camel. Three-color glaze, T'ang Dynasty.

35 Detail of the camel pack. The pack, which hangs down on each side of the camel's back, is shaped to represent a lion's head. On the left of the pack hangs a strip of dried meat such as was eaten during the journey across the desert, and on the right hangs a hose for siphoning water. The water jug, which can be seen in Plate 34 to the right of the hose, is of the handled type popular in the T'ang Dynasty.

36 Woman with a bird. Three-color glaze, T'ang Dynasty, height 21 inches. Many figures with birds perched on their hands are found in this period. Because of their resemblance to Japanese falconers, they are customarily called *takajo* (falconers), though the name is misleading. Parrots and beautiful women are often mentioned in conjunction with each other in T'ang poetry, and this is probably the reason they are depicted together.

37 Woman with a bird. Painted, T'ang Dynasty. This woman, probably a maid or lady in waiting to some

noble, has her hair done up in a double bun and wears a foreign-style robe with turned-down collar, a leather belt, and boots.

38 Woman holding a dog. Painted, T'ang Dynasty, height 19 1/4 inches. The dog which the woman holds is of the breed that later became known as Pekinese, and was imported to Japan to become the ancestor of the Chin, or Japanese spaniel.

39 (*left*) Girl with a Pekinese. Three-color glaze, T'ang Dynasty, height 11 3/4 inches.
(*right*) Woman holding a jar. Three-color glaze, T'ang Dynasty, height 11 5/8 inches. The type of shoes this woman wears, ornamented and turned up sharply in front, are preserved in examples in the Shōsō-in, Nara.

40 Woman with folded hands. Three-color glaze, T'ang Dynasty, height 16 inches. An example of a typical T'ang beauty—such as the one pictured in the Screen Portrait of a Woman in a Feather Dress, preserved in the Shōsō-in—with rouged cheeks and flower patterns painted on her forehead and cheeks.

41 Seated girl with double chignon. Three-color glaze, T'ang Dynasty, height 11 5/8 inches. Chairs were introduced from Central Asia in the Six Dynasties period and, along with the fad for foreign clothes,

were often used in the T'ang. In the following Sung period, foreign dress went out of fashion and there was a return to pure Chinese style, but chairs remained in use.

42,43 Dancers with orchestra. Painted, T'ang Dynasty, height 6–7 inches. Emperor Hsüan Tsung (A.D. 713-756) was extremely fond of singing and dancing and, in a pear garden of his summer palace, supported a trained group of musicians and performers like these, who came to be known as the "Three Thousand Performers of the Pear Garden." The musicians shown here are playing flutes, mouth organs, *p'i-pa* (balloon guitars), and various percussion instruments.

44 Dwarfs (*above*) and camels (*below*). T'ang Dynasty. Collection of Far Eastern Art, Waseda University.

45 Spirit Warrior. Three-color, T'ang Dynasty, height 35 3/8 inches. The black-and-white reproduction of Colorplate 2.

46 Spirit kings guarding a grave. Three-color glaze, T'ang Dynasty.

47 Fabulous animals guarding a grave. Three-color glaze, T'ang Dynasty.

48 "Devil-head" monster. Three-color glaze, T'ang Dynasty, height 42 inches.

3

4

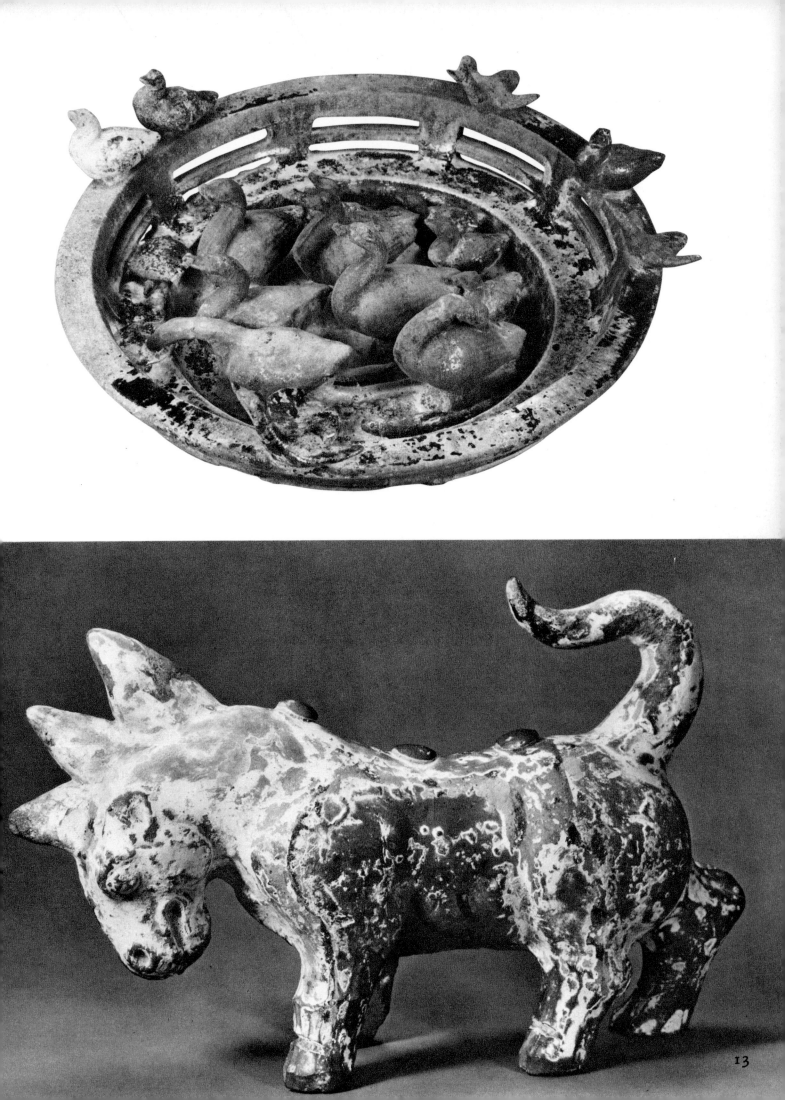

13

15

19

23

31

33

34

39

40

41

44

46

PART II BUDDHIST FIGURES IN BRONZE AND STONE

THOUGH CHINESE society as a whole had already reached a high level of development, both materially and spiritually, by the first century A.D. the religion that prevailed among the common people of the time was apparently a rather primitive and unorganized affair. From what little we know, it appears to have been dominated by shamans and wonder-workers who claimed to be able to cure illness, exorcise evil spirits, foretell the future, and act as mouthpieces for the supernatural. In this folk religion, worship was paid to the ancestors and to certain historical or semihistorical heroes of the past, as well as to various immortal spirits and nature deities; but these last, with a few exceptions, do not bear names that suggest any high degree of anthropomorphism.

Into this society, Buddhism was introduced from India by way of Central Asia. The exact date of its introduction is a matter of conjecture, but reliable sources refer to Buddhist rites and shrines in the time of the Latter Han ruler, Emperor Ming, who reigned from 58 to 75 A.D. Undoubtedly, the foreign religion filtered into China over the trade routes which linked China with the states of Central Asia, and at first flourished mainly, if not exclusively, among the members of the Central Asian communities in the main Chinese cities along the trade routes, from whence it spread gradually throughout Chinese society as a whole. We do not know who were the first monks to propagate the faith; the earliest clearly historical figure we can discern today is the Parthian missionary An Shih-kao, who settled in the Han capital of Lo-yang in A.D. 148.

The early missionaries brought with them Buddhist images, paintings, and scriptures, and in ad-dition to propounding the doctrines of the faith and teaching its meditation techniques to their converts, they devoted much time to the translation of the sacred texts into Chinese, working with the aid of Central Asian interpreters. Educated Chinese, who were heirs to the venerable and sophisticated native philosophical tradition, were not easily attracted to the new religion, many of whose tenets and practices clashed with established Confucian ways. But the masses were more receptive to its appeal, and to win and hold their faith the early missionaries no doubt realized the need for suitably impressive objects of worship. Literary sources indicate that the earliest Buddhist statues were beautiful figures of gilded bronze, but since none have come down to us, we know nothing about their form or style. Figures of Buddhas do occasionally appear on the backs of mirrors dating from about the same period, but these merely replace the representations of mythical beasts or native Chinese deities that customarily ornamented such mirrors; they must be regarded more as good luck charms than as serious objects of worship.

It required considerable time for the foreign missionaries to become fluent in Chinese and for their Chinese converts to master the languages of the Buddhist scriptures. Almost all the early monks whose names are known to us were men of India, or Parthia, or of the smaller states of Central Asia, such as Kucha or Khotan, where Buddhism was already flourishing. Very few Chinese monks are mentioned in sources dealing with the early period.

According to legend, the first Buddhist temple to be built on Chinese soil was the so-called Pai-ma-ssu, or White Horse Temple, of Lo-yang, said to have been founded by monks who came to China

21

from Central Asia in the time of Emperor Ming of the Latter Han. The name of the temple derived from the fact that the missionaries had carried the sacred texts on a white horse during their journey to China. The present-day White Horse Temple is constructed on a high earthen platform, and since such a style of construction is a typical feature of Han architecture, it is not impossible that the structure actually dates, if not from the time of Emperor Ming, at least from a period not too far removed from the reputed date of its founding.

In the *San Kuo Chih*[8] (Record of the Three Kingdoms) we read of one Chai Jung, who built a shrine at Hsü-chou in present-day Kiangsu, consisting of a multistoried pagoda and a hall, in which he placed a gilded bronze Buddha clothed in brocade. This is one of the few clues we have to the nature of these early Buddhist shrines. Chai Jung died in 195; the building of the shrines seems to have taken place a few years before his death.

The *Hou Han Chi* (Chronicles of the Latter Han) by Yüan Hung (d. 376), in its account of the introduction of Buddhism into China (Emperor Ming 13th year; A.D. 70), describes Buddhist figures as being "one *chang* six *ch'ih* in height, golden in color, and with a nimbus fixed to the back of the neck." One *chang* is equal to ten *ch'ih*, and the *ch'ih* of late Han times, the period which Yüan Hung is describing, was about 9 inches long, so that the figures were probably about twice life size. From this it would appear that not only miniature figures but life-size or larger-than-life-size figures as well were already in use in China.

Early Indian Buddhists did not employ images of the Buddha as objects of devotion, but instead worshiped symbols of his presence, such as the Wheel of the Law, the lotus, the bo tree, or the stupa. The earliest representations of Buddhas and bodhisattvas date from the first century B.C., and were produced mainly in the region of Gandhāra in western Pakistan. Gandhāra had earlier been under Greek control, and though rulership eventually passed into Indian hands, the influence of Greek culture remained strong in the area and is clearly reflected in the Buddhist sculpture produced there, executed in the so-called Gandhāran style.

This style was transmitted to the Buddhist states of Central Asia, and from there introduced into China. Practically no example of Buddhist images survives that can be reliably dated to the Latter Han, Three Kingdoms, or Western Chin times, i.e., to the period prior to 317. From the period of disunion that followed, however, when a succession of native Chinese dynasties ruled the south, and northern China was split up among the so-called Sixteen States, we find a few isolated examples of gilded bronze images in the Gandhāran style (see Plate 35). The earliest that bears a dated inscription is a small figure, executed in rather crude style, from the Hsia state on the western border of China, dated 429. Next earliest is the figure shown in Plate 36, a product of the Liu Sung Dynasty of the south, dated 437. Other examples, belonging to the Northern Wei Dynasty (386–534) and bearing dates of the T'ai-p'ing-chen-chün era (440–450), are extant.

A glance at these images from the early period shows that the treatment of the drapery follows Gandhāran style exactly. In the modeling of the face, however, there is a departure from Gandhāran style, the features of the northern images being even more masculine and powerful than those of the typical Gandhāran figure; those of the south tend toward a softer, more feminine appearance, a difference that suggests the contrast between the stern, militaristic society of the northern states, dominated by alien conquerors and monks, and the more refined, aristocratic culture of the native Chinese dynasties of the south.

It required many years for Buddhism to spread beyond the first urban centers of missionary activity and to penetrate Chinese society on a large scale. The earliest missionaries, as we have seen, devoted much of their time to the translation and exegesis of the sacred texts, and this activity was greatly accelerated during the years of national unity under the Western Chin Dynasty (265–316). Toward the end of this period, Buddhism began to

---

[8] *Chüan* 49, the biography of Liu Yao.

exercise a significant influence among the educated classes, who were attracted to it because of its apparent similarities to the philosophy of the "Dark Learning," or Neo-Taoism, which had come to enjoy great popularity at this time. In their eyes Buddhist thought, particularly that of the Mahayana schools, appeared to deal with the same metaphysical problems that occupied the Neo-Taoist thinkers, such as the nature of wisdom, quietude, and the void; therefore it was the philosophy of the new religion, rather than its devotional aspects, which captured the interest of the learned Chinese. The apparent similarities between Taoist and Buddhist philosophy were rendered even more striking by the fact that the early translators of Buddhist texts drew heavily upon Taoist terminology in rendering the philosophical vocabulary of the new religion into Chinese.

At the same time, however, Buddhism introduced two strikingly new elements into traditional Chinese thought: the doctrine of karma, according to which the moral actions of the individual during his lifetime automatically determine the nature of his life after death; and the doctrine of rebirth, which the Chinese at first mistakenly understood as a doctrine of the immortality of the individual soul. Gradually, as the complex and lofty philosophy of Buddhism was transmitted and interpreted to the Chinese, it began to attract followers from the educated gentry as well as from the common people, and Buddhism for the first time became an influential part of Chinese culture.

The Chin court was forced by barbarian invasions to flee south in 316 and to establish a new capital at the location of present-day Nanking. Buddhism continued, after the move, to spread among the aristocracy and gentry of the south, many of whom had fled from the north along with the court, and in 381 it attained an unprecedented level of esteem when, for the first time in history, a Chinese monarch, Emperor Hsiao-wu of the Eastern Chin, after years of generous patronage, publicly proclaimed himself a lay follower of the new religion. In addition to the court-centered Buddhism of the southern aristocracy, several important monastic centers were established, such as that founded by Tao-an (312–385) at Hsiang-yang in present Hupeh, and that of Hui-yüan (334–417) at Mount Lu in present Kiangsi. These centers attracted many brilliant young men who, repelled by the dangerous and unsavory political atmosphere of the time, chose to live in the seclusion of the monastic community and devote their lives to study and meditation.

Meanwhile, among the alien-controlled states of the north, Buddhism made even more rapid progress, for it did not have to contend with a firmly entrenched Confucian theory of government or the age-old Chinese prejudice against foreign beliefs and customs. The illiterate barbarian rulers of the north seem to have been attracted to Buddhism initially by its superstitious and miracle-working aspects, finding in it resemblances to the shamanism with which they were already familiar. The new religion also appealed to them because it created a bond among the heterogeneous ethnic groups who had settled in northern China during this period, and with the peoples of the Central Asian states with whom North China traded. The rulers accordingly bestowed great honors upon the more eminent missionaries and clergymen, such as the Indian monk Fo-t'u-teng of the early fourth century. The most powerful of these northern states, the Northern Wei, founded by the T'o-pa Turks in 385 and by 440 in the control of almost all of northern China, was, as we shall see, particularly lavish in its patronage of Buddhism. Much of the finest Chinese Buddhist sculpture dates from the time of its rule.

CAVE TEMPLES

THE FAMOUS Buddhist caves of Ajanta in India and the caves and colossal images at Bahmiyan in Afghanistan were carved out of the living rock of the cliff faces, and this same technique of carving Buddhist temples and images was attempted in the states of Central Asia into which Buddhism spread. The region of Central Asia, however, lacks stone of good quality; the best it possesses is a coarse sandstone which, though it can be hollowed into caves, is not good enough for sculpture, and so images were made of a wooden core to which was applied a stucco coating made of clay and plant fibers. When completed, the figures were painted in lifelike colors. Because of the perishable nature of the materials used, however, no examples of such stucco figures form the early period survive today.

The Caves of the Thousand Buddhas of Tun-huang, situated about twelve miles southeast of the city of Tun-huang in western Kansu, have become world famous since the discovery there in 1900 of a priceless store of ancient Buddhist paintings and texts, written in Chinese and the various languages of India and Central Asia. Tun-huang, formerly the region of Sha-chou, is situated at the western gateway to China, and it was an important stopping place for travelers and trade caravans passing back and forth over the Silk Road. Construction of the caves began in 366 at the request of a monk named Lo-tsun, and was carried on for the following thousand years, until the time of the Yüan Dynasty. At present, over 480 caves of various sizes are still in existence. All of the Buddhist figures in these caves are made of stucco and painted in a variety of colors, and the walls and ceilings of the caves are covered with murals and decorative motifs. The whole effect is one of almost indescribable brilliance and splendor, and it no doubt filled the hearts of the pilgrims who flocked there from many lands with awe and wonder. Not many of the original stucco figures that filled the caves exist today, but examples can be found which date from the Northern Wei, Western Wei, Sui, T'ang, and Five Dynasties periods. Some are of great size, such as the Buddha of Cave 130, dated 713, which is 85 feet high, the head alone being 24 feet.

The caves of Mai-chi-shan, situated on the upper reaches of the Wei River in T'ien-shui-hsien in Kansu, have long been famous in the history of Chinese Buddhism and have become well-known to art scholars of the world as a result of an archaeological survey carried out there in 1953. It is not certain when they were first begun, though a monk named Hsüan-kao (d. 446) is said to have visited the spot in 420 and, with another monk who resided there, to have trained a group of more than three hundred disciples. It would appear from this, therefore, that the caves were already functioning as a religious center by the end of the fourth or the beginning of the fifth century.

The stone of which the caves are constructed is of poor quality, and there are therefore many stucco figures; but since the site was nearer to the center of China than Tun-huang, stone figures and stele could be carved elsewhere and transported to Mai-chi-shan, to be placed in the caves or set in niches in the rock walls. Among such stucco figures are specimens dating from the Northern Wei, Sui, T'ang, and Sung periods. The caves are cut into the face of a sheer cliff; to provide access it was necessary to drill holes in the rock, insert timbers, and construct a wooden pathway projecting from the cliff. In some cases, buildings were constructed in front of the caves; their supports likewise had to be made of timbers inserted in holes in the rock.

Another well-known group of caves in Kansu is that of Ping-ling-ssu, on the upper waters of the Yellow River in Yung-ch'ing-hsien. These caves bear an inscription in stone with a date equivalent to 513, so it is certain that their construction began sometime before that. There are twelve caves and niches dating from the Northern Wei, twenty-one caves and eighty-five niches dating from the T'ang, and five caves and one niche dating from the Ming Dynasty, making a total of 124 caves and niches. The niches are scooped out of the cliff and are no more than shallow indentations for the stone images, so that the figures can be easily seen from the exterior. Such niches, needless to say, are easier to construct than caves, and the large number of them found at Ping-ling-ssu constitutes one of the distinctive features of the site.

The famous caves of Yün-kang are located ten miles west of the Northern Wei capital of P'ing-ch'eng (present-day Ta-t'ung) in Shansi, in the cliff along the Wu-chou River. The Northern Wei dynasty was founded by T'o-pa Turks who had formerly inhabited the region of Inner Mongolia. Taking advantage of the chaotic political situation in northern China, they moved south of the Great Wall, and in 386 their leader, T'o-pa Kuei, assumed the title of King of Wei. In 396, after gaining control of present-day Shansi and Hopeh provinces, he changed his title to Emperor and established his capital at P'ing-ch'eng. T'o-pa Kuei, better known by his posthumous title of T'ai-tsu Tao-wu, was a Buddhist believer, and he had a number of temples constructed in the capital. He also summoned the eminent monk Fa-kuo to his court and honored him with the title of Comptroller of Religions.

For a time Buddhism prospered under the patronage of the new dynasty, but in 440 the third ruler, Emperor T'ai-wu, acting on the advice of Taoist ministers, adopted a Taoist-era name, and shortly thereafter began a persecution of the foreign religion that culminated in an edict of 446, ordering the destruction of all Buddhist temples, images, and scriptures, and the execution of the clergy. As a result, many religious buildings were actually demolished, though most of the clergy were able to escape into hiding and to conceal a large portion of the sacred images and texts. Emperor T'ai-wu was assassinated by a courtier in 452, and his successor, Emperor Wen-ch'eng, immediately rescinded the proscription against Buddhists and appointed the Indian monk Shi-hsien to the post of Comptroller of Religions.

When Shih-hsien died early in the Ho-p'ing era (460-466), he was succeeded by another eminent monk, T'an-yao, and the title of the office was changed to Comptroller of Monks. T'an-yao worked to restore Buddhism to the flourishing state it had enjoyed before the persecution, and one of his acts was to petition the Emperor for permission to have five caves constructed on the bank of the Wu-chou River and furnished with colossal stone images in honor of the Emperor and four of his predecessors. The caves that were constructed as a result, known as T'an-yao's caves, correspond to the sixteenth and twentieth of the present series of Yün-kang caves, each with a stone Buddha measuring from 42 to more than 52 feet in height.

In addition to these, a number of other caves of various sizes were constructed, including a group of twenty-one caves situated a little more than a mile away from the main site, all decorated with countless carved images in high and low relief. After the Northern Wei Dynasty moved its capital from P'ing-ch'eng to Lo-yang in 493, however, the caves fell into neglect, and remained almost forgotten until the present century, when the beauty of their sculpture at last won them the recognition they deserve (Plate 9).

In 495, two years after the capital was moved to Lo-yang, work was begun on a new series of caves known as the Lung-men Caves. They are situated about eight miles south of the present city of Lo-yang, at a site where the Yi River runs through a narrow mountain defile. The spot was known from ancient times as Teng-lung-men, or the Ascending Dragon Gate, and the caves take their name from the last two characters of this old designation. They are hollowed in the rock base of the mountains on either side of the river. Construction continued at the site for the following four centuries, during the Western Wei, Northern Ch'i, Northern Chou, Sui, and T'ang dynasties, and at the present time 1,352 caves of various sizes as well as 785 small niches remain. No less than 97,306 images have been counted at the site, 3,680 of which bear inscriptions. The cave known as the Ku-yang-tung, which was completed in 575, contains a number of works of the Northern Wei period, and nineteen of the twenty most famous inscriptions of Lung-men.

The Pin-yang-tung, one of two caves constructed in memory of Emperor Hsiao-wen and his consort, Empress Dowager Wen-chao, was begun in 500 and required twenty-four years to complete. It is said that 102,366 workmen were engaged in its construction. The main image is a seated figure of Sakyamuni, 27 feet high, flanked by two figures on either side; in addition, there are two groups of three bodhisattva figures each, grouped on the left and right, making a total of eleven large figures, as well as numerous wall carvings.

The cave known as the Feng-hsien-ssu is a representative work of the T'ang Dynasty, and dates from 672 to 675. The wooden temple structure that once fronted it is no longer in existence, and the cave lies open to view, presenting a truly impressive sight to the visitor. The central figure is a seated image of Variochana, 59 feet high, flanked by two standing bodhisattvas on either side. Images of the four Guardian Kings are carved in high relief on the side walls of the cave, two on each side, and the areas between the figures are filled with smaller carved Buddhist images. There are numerous other important caves at the Lung-men site, among them the famous Lien-hua-tung and Yao-fang-tung, and small stone figures even crowd the road along the river. The magnificent head of a guardian king, (Plate 24), which dates from the T'ang Dynasty, was taken from the Lung-men site.

Also dating from the Northern Wei Dynasty are five caves and a large stone Buddha situated at Kung-hsien in Honan (Plates 8 and 11-13). In Shansi, near the city of T'ai-yüan, are the twenty-four caves of the T'ien-lung-shan group, dating mostly from the Northern Ch'i (550-577) (Plate 29). Largely from the same period are the two groups of caves at Hsiang-t'ang-shan in Hopeh, a southern group of seven caves situated in Tz'u-hsien, and a northern group of the same number in Wu-an-hsien (Plate 19). The stone caves of Yü-han-shan and Yün-men in Shantung date from the Sui Dynasty (581-618), as well as most of the caves of T'o-shan in the same province. In addition, a number of caves have recently been discovered in western China, in the region of Szechwan.

Needless to say, stone images are found not only in cave temples such as have been described above, but as free-standing figures decorating the exteriors of ordinary temples as well. These free-standing figures, however, are never more than 10 feet in height, and most of them measure only about a foot. Some are made of very high-quality stone, such as the white marble figures of the Northern Ch'i and T'ang periods (Colorplate I, Plates 18-21 and 39), or the Northern Chou figures executed in fine yellow limestone (Plate 22).

DURING THE Northern Wei period, the magnificent cave temples which we have discussed were constructed at Yün-kang, Lung-men, and other sites. The center of Buddhist activity, however, was not at these sites, but in the two Wei capitals. By 477, we are told, the temples in the earlier Northern Wei capital of P'ing-ch'eng numbered nearly one hundred, with over two thousand monks and nuns attending them. They were built and maintained by the generous alms of the emperors and the aristocracy, and were undoubtedly most impressive structures. Though P'ing-ch'eng was situated far on the northern border, it appears from descriptions to have been a city of gorgeous palaces and temples (Plates 1-13).

After the Northern Wei Dynasty moved its capital to Lo-yang, Buddhism enjoyed even greater honor and affluence. According to the *Lo-yang Ch'ieh-lan Chi*, an account of the temples of the capital, written by Yang Hsüan-chih around 547, there were 1,367 temples in the city, adorned with images made of bronze, wood, dried lacquer, clay, and stone, and painted with gold (Plates 14-17). The custom of gilding Buddhist images existed in India and the states of Central Asia, and is frequently mentioned in the accounts of Chinese pilgrims to those lands. In China, gilded images, as we have seen, are mentioned as early as the Latter Han Dynasty, and as Chinese society increased in opulence, they were made in ever larger numbers.

The *Lo-yang Ch'ieh-lan Chi* contains descriptions of such images. In relating the origin of the Kuang-ming-ssu, one of the smaller temples of Lo-yang, the first chapter of the work states that a certain Tuan Hui, magistrate of Pao-hsin-hsien, having heard voices and seen strange lights in his house, dug up the ground under it and found a golden Buddha measuring three *ch'ih*, attended by two bodhisattvas. The image bore an inscription with the date "Chin Dynasty, T'ai-shih era 2nd year, 5th month, 15th day," which corresponds to A.D. 266. Tuan Hui accordingly converted his home

26

into a temple for the worship of the image. Since Buddhism was already known in this area by the year 266, it is quite possible that the statue which he found actually dated from that time.

In connection with the Yung-ning-ssu, the work states, in the same chapter, that it was founded in 516 by the Empress Dowager Ling, and that it contained a nine-story pagoda measuring 90 *chang* in height, to the north of which stood a magnificent hall modeled after one of the imperial halls of state. Within the hall stood a golden Buddha 8 *chang* in height, ten life-size golden figures, three figures adorned with pearls, five figures clothed in gold cloth, and two made of precious stones. All the scriptures and images presented by foreign states were said to have been kept in this temple.

In the section on the P'ing-teng-ssu, in the second chapter, the work mentions a gilded statue measuring 2 *chang* 8 *ch'ih* in height, which was so large that it had to be placed outside the temple gate. Whenever some unusual occurrence was about to take place in the state, the statue was said to have wept, and at such times the citizens would gather in great haste to observe it. According to the third chapter of the same work, on the day before the festival of the Buddha's birthday, which was held on the eighth day of the fourth month, over a thousand statues from the various temples in the city were brought together at the Ching-ming-ssu, south of the city wall, and on the following day they were carried in procession to the front of the palace, where the Emperor scattered flowers over them.

The *Lo-yang Ch'ieh-lan Chi* gives many other details which help us visualize the flourishing state of the Buddhist temples in the city under the Northern Wei Dynasty; but today, with the exception of the White Horse Temple west of the old wall, all have vanished and nothing remains but a few broken tiles scattered about the open fields.

Since the gilded bronze figures were, with a few exceptions such as the large figure described above, customarily placed on altars in the temple interiors, they were usually quite small. Of those that remain in existence, the largest measures around 10 inches in height, while some are as small as 2 ½ inches (Plates 35–47). The pedestals of the figures ordinarily bear inscriptions giving the date and the name of the donor or donors, as will be seen in Plate 39. Small stone images also bear inscriptions of the same nature. In addition, small clay figures that could be produced easily from molds began to be popular from Northern Wei times on, though most of the extant examples date from the T'ang Dynasty. Of far greater artistic merit are the gilded panels of hammered bronze reliefs, such as are shown in Colorplate 2 and Plate 47. Here, in a single panel about 6 inches square, are depicted a Buddha seated on an elaborate pedestal and attended by bodhisattvas, arhats, guardian deities, and flying angels, all executed with superb skill.

OUTLINE OF STYLISTIC FEATURES BY PERIODS

BUDDHIST images underwent numerous stylistic changes during the long history of Buddhism on Chinese soil. As we have noted above, the first images to be introduced to China from Central Asia were executed in the Gandhāran style. The successive styles may be conveniently summarized as follows:

Archaic. The eyes are open and a small moustache slants downward on the upper lip. The hands are large in proportion to the body, and the robe, with its numerous folds, is done in the style typical of Gandhāran pieces. The nimbus is not yet extensively developed. The whole figure tends to have a rather stern appearance. Both seated and standing figures are depicted. (Plate 35.)

Northern Dynasties, early period (up to the time of Yün-kang caves). Examples dating from the T'ai-p'ing chen-chün era (440–450) still retain many characteristics of the archaic style. The hands sometimes show the webs between the fingers, one of the thirty-two physical marks of the Buddha. The pedestal is Chinese in style and inscribed. The face begins to show a resemblance to the physical types of the northern tribes, but, perhaps due to the presence of numerous foreign missionaries during the period, it has not yet developed

27

a distinctively Chinese cast (Plates 1, 2, 3, and 6).

Southern Dynasties. Judging from a few specimens dating from the Yüan-chia era (424-453) of the Liu Sung Dynasty, the Buddhist figures produced by the Chinese living in the region of the Yangtze Valley had acquired the gentle, rounded faces of typical Chinese. The nimbus differs in form between north and south. That of the southern figures is particularly well developed and is often marked with a flame-like design. (Plate 36.)

Northern Dynasties, Yün-kang period (460-493). Influenced by the earlier northern style, the images of the Yün-kang period are marked by stocky, well-rounded figures and masculine features typical of the races of the north. The eyes are half closed, and the folds of the dangling robe tend to be short.

Northern Dynasties, Lung-men period (494-550). The rulers of the Northern Wei Dynasty, having become increasingly Sinicized, moved their capital to Lo-yang in 493, and the change is reflected in the Buddhist figures of the succeeding Lung-men period. They become less stern and more sumptuous in style, while the faces and bodies take on a slim, elongated form suggestive of divine mystery. The dangling folds of the robe become longer and more decorative in treatment. (Plates 8-17.)

Northern Ch'i, Northern Chou, and Sui periods (551-618). During this period the elongated figures of the Lung-men period give way to plump, youthful figures marked by much greater realism. The folds of the robe become short and conventionalized in form (Plates 18-23). Very few works dating from the late southern courts of the Ch'i, Liang, and Ch'en dynasties are extant, probably because most of them were executed in wood or dry lacquer. By this time all important stylistic differences between north and south had disappeared.

T'ang period (619-907). The most important sculpture of the T'ang Dynasty dates from its early years—the period known as the height of the T'ang (684-755)—after which there is a definite decline in the level of artistic merit. The T'ang figures are marked by a continuation of the preceding Northern Ch'i, Northern Chou, and Sui style. The faces become fuller and more grave, with small full-lipped mouths, and the figures as a whole acquire an air of solemnity and compassion. The dangling folds of the robe are simplified until they become merely a decorative covering for the pedestal. Whereas in earlier centuries most of the images had been representations of Sakyamuni or Maitreya, by the T'ang times these deities are joined by a variety of other Buddhas and bodhisattvas (Plate 28), such as Vairochana, Amida, Avalokitesvara, and Ksitigarbha. It is interesting to note, however, that, although images of Acalanatha, or Fudō Myōō, are extremely common in early Japanese esoteric Buddhism, they are almost unknown in China. (Colorplate 1, Plates 24-27, and 29-34.)

Sung period (960-1279). During much of the Sung period, the northern part of China was under the control of the Tartar states of Liao and Chin. In the Buddhist figures of this period, the tendency is toward greater realism, particularly in the bodhisattva figures, with their doll-like faces. The Ch'an sect, which places little emphasis upon the worship of images, was the dominant school of Buddhism, and there was accordingly a decline of interest in the making of Buddha figures. Artists instead applied themselves to the creation of lifelike statues of Ch'an patriarchs and arhats, executed in dry lacquer or wood. (Plate 48.)

28

Part Two: Commentaries on the Plates

COLORPLATES

1 Seated Buddha, from the Ch'ing-lung-ssu in Ch'ang-an (present-day Sian, Shensi). White marble; T'ang Dynasty; height of figure 23 3/8 inches, total height 29 inches. Collection Hosokawa Goryu.

2 Buddha panel. Gilded bronze; Northern Wei Dynasty; height 6 3/8 inches, width 4 1/2 inches.

3 Detail of seated Buddha (see Plate 4).

BLACK–AND–WHITE PLATES

1 Standing Buddha, from Cho-hsien, Hopeh. Sandstone; Northern Wei Dynasty, early period; height of figure 6 feet 6 inches, total height 12 feet. Okura Museum of Antiquities, Tokyo.

2 Seated Buddha. Sandstone; Northern Wei Dynasty, A.D. 455; height 14 inches. Fujii Museum of Chinese Antiquities, Kyoto.

3 Reverse side of Plate 2.

4 Seated Buddha with two attendants, from Sian, Shensi. Sandstone, Northern Wei Dynasty, height 17 7/8 inches.

5 Reverse side of Plate 4.

6 Seated Buddha. Sandstone; Northern Wei Dynasty, A.D. 457; height 16 1/4 inches.

7 Maitreya bodhisattva in meditation with left leg pendent, from Sian, Shensi. Yellow limestone, Northern Wei Dynasty, height 25 1/8 inches. Collection Hosokawa Goryu.

8 Head of a standing bodhisattva, from Kung-hsien, Honan. Sandstone, Northern Wei Dynasty, height 16 1/8 inches.

9 Head of a Buddha, from Yün-kang, Shansi. Sandstone, Northern Wei dynasty, height 15 1/2 inches.

10 Trinity of Taoist figures. Sandstone; Northern Wei Dynasty, A.D. 508-512; height 20 1/4 inches.

11 Figures of donors, from Kung-hsien, Honan. Sandstone, Northern Wei Dynasty, height 18 inches.

12, 13 Group of donors, Kung-hsien, Honan. Sandstone, Northern Wei Dynasty, height 13 3/4 inches.

14 Maitreya bodhisattva in meditation with left leg pendent. White marble; Eastern Wei Dynasty, A.D. 544; height 21 3/8 inches. Shodō Museum, Tokyo.

15 Group of Buddhist figures. Yellow limestone; Eastern Wei Dynasty, A.D. 538; height 26 1/8 inches. Fujii Museum of Chinese Antiquities, Kyoto.

16, 17 Buddha with two attendants. Limestone; Eastern Wei Dynasty, A.D. 535; height of figures 37 inches, total height 70 inches. Fujii Museum of Chinese Antiquities, Kyoto.

18. Head of a standing Buddha. White marble; Northern Ch'i Dynasty, A.D. 564; height of the Buddha 4 feet 5 inches, total height of the sculpture 7 feet 5 inches. Fujii Museum of Chinese Antiquities, Kyoto.

19 Head of a bodhisattva, from Hsiang-t'ang-shan, Hopeh. White marble, Northern Ch'i Dynasty, height 12 3/4 inches.

20 Buddha with four attendants under a tree. White marble, Northern Ch'i Dynasty, height 18 1/8 inches.

21 Bodhisattva with leg pendent. White marble, Northern Ch'i Dynasty, height 13 3/4 inches.

22 Standing bodhisattva. Yellow limestone; Northern Chou Dynasty, A.D. 566; height 17 1/2 inches.

23 Standing Avalokitesvara bodhisattva. Yellow limestone; Sui Dynasty, A.D. 600; height 15 inches.

24 Head of a Guardian King, from Lung-men, Honan. Sandstone, T'ang Dynasty, height 16 5/8 inches.

25 Seated Buddha. Limestone; T'ang Dynasty, A.D. 639; height 32 inches. Fujii Museum of Chinese Antiquities, Kyoto.

26. Seated Buddha. Limestone; T'ang Dynasty, A.D. 689; height of figure 9 1/2 inches, total height 16 1/2 inches.

27 Seated Buddha. Limestone; T'ang Dynasty, A.D. 711; total height 49 inches. Shodō Museum, Tokyo.

28 Head of bodhisattva. Sandstone, Northern Wei Dynasty.

29 Head of bodhisattva, from T'ien-lung-shan, Shansi. Sandstone, height of head 11 3/4 inches. Nezu Art Museum, Tokyo.

29

30 Standing Avalokitesvara with eleven heads, from the Pao-ch'ing-ssu, Ch'ang-an. Limestone, T'ang Dynasty, total height 41 inches. Collection Hosokawa Goryu.

31 Stele with seated Buddha in niche, from the Pao-ch'ing-ssu, Ch'ang-an. Limestone, T'ang Dynasty, height 42 1/4 inches. Collection Hosokawa Goryu.

32 Standing Ksitigarbha bodhisattva. White marble, T'ang Dynasty, height 14 1/2 inches.

33 Seated Buddha, from the Ch'ing-lung-ssu, Ch'ang-an. White marble; T'ang Dynasty; height of figure 23 1/2 inches, total height 29 inches.

34 Stele of a thousand Buddhas. T'ang Dynasty, height 23 1/2 inches.

35 Archaic-style standing bodhisattva. Gilded bronze, late third to early fourth century, height 13 1/8 inches. Fujii Museum of Chinese Antiquities, Kyoto.

36 Seated Buddha. Gilded bronze; Liu Sung Dynasty, A.D. 437; height of figures 8 5/8 inches, total height 11 1/2 inches.

37 Seated Buddha. Gilded Bronze, Northern Wei Dynasty, height 7 3/8 inches.

38 Two seated Buddhas. Gilded bronze; Northern Wei Dynasty, A.D. 489; height 9 1/4 inches. Nezu Art Museum, Tokyo.

39 Reverse side of Plate 38.

40 (left) Standing figure. Gilded bronze; Northern Wei Dynasty, A.D. 493; height of figure 4 1/8 inches, total height 9 1/4 inches. (right) Standing figure. Gilded bronze; Northern Wei Dynasty, A.D. 483; height 12 inches.

41 (left) Standing bodhisattva holding a lotus. Gilded bronze; Northern Wei Dynasty, A.D. 471; height of figure 4 5/8 inches. (right) Standing figure. Gilded bronze; Northern Wei Dynasty, A.D. 484; height 8 5/8 inches.

42 Standing Buddha. Gilded bronze; Northern Wei Dynasty, A.D. 526. Fujii Museum of Chinese Antiquities, Kyoto.

43 Standing Buddha with two attendants. Gilded bronze; Northern Wei Dynasty, A.D. 532. Nezu Art Museum, Tokyo.

44 Standing Buddha with two attendants, detail of central figure. Bronze; Northern Wei Dynasty, A.D. 522; height of figure 10 1/4 inches. Fujii Museum of Chinese Antiquities, Kyoto.

45 Standing Buddha with two attendants, detail of right attendant (see Plate 44). Height 13 inches.

46 Standing Buddha with four attendants. Gilded bronze, Eastern Wei Dynasty, height 9 inches.

47 Buddha. Gilded bronze, hammered relief; Sui Dynasty; height 6 1/2 inches. Collection Hosokawa Goryu.

48 Standing Buddha. Gilded bronze; Sung Dynasty; height of figure 28 1/2 inches, total height 33 1/2 inches.

2

4

20

21

26

33

39

40

43

45

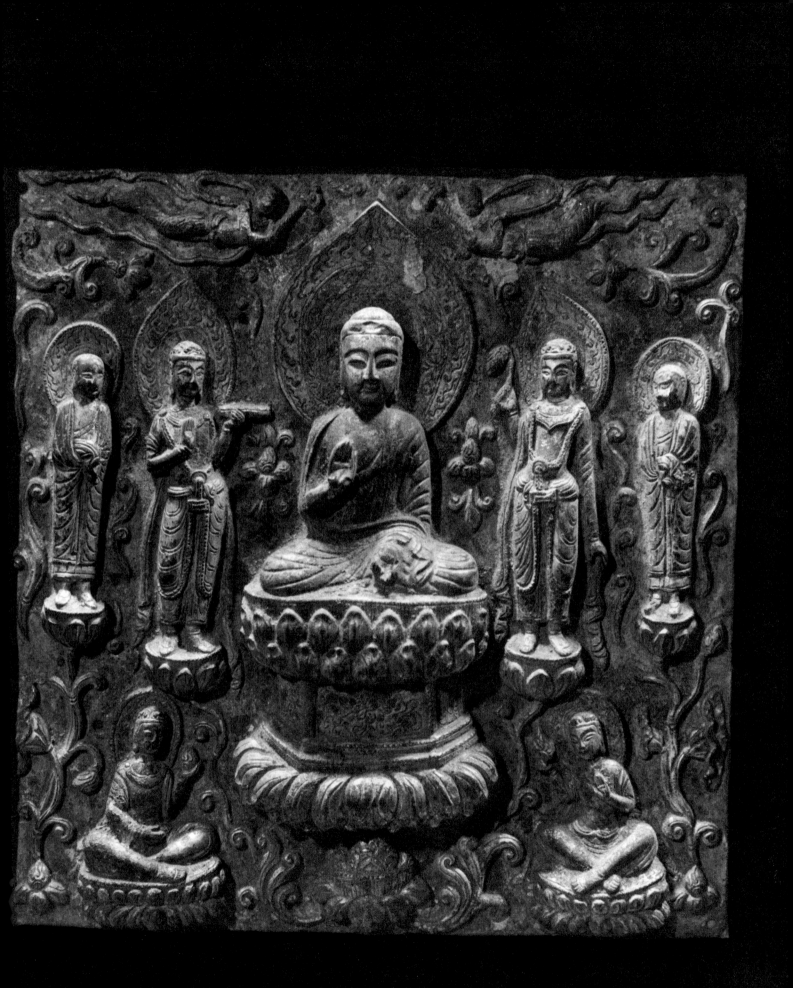

PART III BRONZES AND JADES

A BRONZE CULTURE made its first appearance in East Asia among the Chinese who lived and farmed on the great plains around the lower reaches of the Yellow River. The date of its appearance seems to be about the fifteenth century B.C. It was preceded by the so-called Yang-shao culture, centered in western China and characterized by red-painted pottery, as described in Part I, and by the Lung-shan culture of the eastern seaboard, characterized by black pottery. But, although each of these cultures produced pottery of superior design and workmanship, neither developed the use of bronze. It has been suggested that the technique of bronze casting was introduced to China from the Near East, but no evidence has been found to prove this assertion, and it seems questionable in view of the fact that the forms of the earliest bronze vessels are distinctly Chinese, and obviously derive directly from the pottery of the preceding culture.

Traditional accounts of ancient Chinese history describe an early age of culture heroes and sage rulers, followed by the Hsia Dynasty, the Shang or Yin Dynasty, and the Chou Dynasty, commonly referred to as the Three Dynasties. Since the earliest written accounts of antiquity we possess today were compiled and edited during the Chou Dynasty, they may be regarded as reasonably reliable when dealing with Chou history. Until recently we had no way to test the validity of their accounts of the preceding Shang Dynasty and their list of Shang rulers.

Early Chinese bronzes often bear inscriptions and, though they were not scientifically excavated until the present century, in the past they often came to light accidentally, so that Chinese scholars from the eleventh century on began making systematic collections of ancient bronzes and studying their inscriptions. Since these scholars lacked other means of dating the bronzes, it was the custom among them to attribute pieces with short inscriptions to the Shang Dynasty, and those with longer inscriptions to the Chou. But, except for such tentative pieces of evidence, until recent times there was no archaeological proof of the existence of the Shang Dynasty.

Around the beginning of the present century, however, as mentioned in Part I, inscribed oracle bones from An-yang, the site of the last Shang capital, began to attract the notice of scholars. The inscriptions on these bones, when deciphered, provided independent proof of the existence of the Shang Dynasty, and even corroborated the list of Shang rulers preserved in the traditional written accounts. Moreover, as a result of the systematic excavations carried out at the An-yang site since 1928, it is now possible to date the ancient bronzes with a reasonable degree of certainty.

The objects discovered at the An-yang site reveal that the society of late Shang times had attained a much higher level of cultural development than the scholars had hitherto supposed. Lo Chen-yü, one of the pioneers in the deciphering of the oracle bone inscriptions, noted that the bronzes with long inscriptions, which date from Chou times, were of cruder workmanship than those with brief inscriptions or no inscriptions at all, which date from Shang times. In other words, contrary to what might be expected, the level of bronze workmanship was higher in the Shang period than in the succeeding Chou. But if this is so, then there must have been a period of crude and experimental workmanship that preceded the high

37

level attained in late Shang times. Until very recently no remains from this earlier period had been found. In 1950, however, the site of a Shang Dynasty city was discovered in Cheng-chou in Honan, probably the site of the city called Ao, which is mentioned in literary sources as the capital of the tenth ruler of the dynasty.

Since that time, a number of other Shang-period sites have been discovered, many of them predating the An-yang site; and the bronzes recovered from these, as might be expected, are cruder in form and technique than those of An-yang. Crucibles and sectional molds used in their production also have been found, so that we now know much about how the bronze vessels were cast. In addition to vessels, it is clear that bronze spearheads, knives, dagger-axes, chisels, and other tools were being produced by this time, estimated to be around the fourteenth century B.C.

The Shang rulers sought the advice of their ancestors in all their undertakings. Through the medium of shaman diviners, they consulted the spirit world on matters pertaining to warfare, travel, sacrifices, hunts, the harvest, and even the weather, and then acted according to the favorable or unfavorable answers received. Sacrifices had to be offered constantly to these ancestors, as well as to various nature deities, and at these ceremonies food and drink were offered to the spirits as though to living persons. For such occasions,' vessels of a special and sacrosanct nature were needed; these were cast in bronze, the most precious metal of the time. In form, they were imitations of the pottery vessels used for everyday eating and drinking.

A word should be said here about the various forms of these vessels. The *li* vessel, which is exclusive to China, is distinguished by its three hollow legs. In earlier times, vessels with pointed bottoms had been used, and it is probable that the *li* form was suggested by the sight of three of these vessels leaning together over a fire. Similar to the *li* is the *ting*, or tripod. Its legs, unlike those of the *li*, are not hollow, but are long and thin, raising the pot up above the fire and allowing the air to circulate under it. Both forms evolved first in pottery and were later imitated in bronze.

The *hsien*, or steamer, another pottery form, consists of a *li* with a perforated lid, on top of which is placed a second pot. Water is put in the lower part and grain in the upper part, where it is cooked by the steam, as in a double boiler. The *chüeh* is a kind of drinking cup provided with a long spout and three legs so that it can be set directly over the fire for heating wine (Plates 8, 9, 24, and 25). The *tsun* (Plates 16, 17 left and right, and 26–31) is also a container for wine. The character *tsun* (尊) was originally a picture of two hands holding up such a wine vessel, from which in time it acquired the meaning of "worthy" or "venerable." The *ku*, another wine cup, is in the form of an inverted horn with a base attached to the tip. It derives from the drinking horns of ancient times. Another wine vessel, the *yu*, is often provided with a bail handle, and hence is known as a *t'i-liang yu*, or "bail-handled *yu*" (Plates 1, 7, 12, 13, 20, and 33). There are other types of wine vessels with handles, such as the *kuang* (Plate 18, lower section), the *ho* (Plate 32), or the *chia* (Plate 5), as well as vessels for food, such as the *kuei* (Plate 18, lower section), which derives its form from a basket of woven bamboo.

These various types of sacrificial vessels were cast in bronze and decorated with elaborate designs. Since they were to be used for sacred services, however, the artist was not free to employ any design that took his fancy but was confined to certain motifs with magical or religious significance. The most common motif is that of the *t'ao-t'ieh*, already mentioned in Part I, a representation of an animal face that was apparently intended to drive away evil spirits. Actually, the term *t'ao-t'ieh* covers a wide variety of representations on these early bronzes. Some of the heads have horns which resemble those of an ox; others have the curved horns of a ram, or the bottle-shaped horns that are associated in Chinese lore with the dragon. The features of the face are treated in a highly abstract manner, the powerful eyes and mouth forming the focal point of the design. Examples of *t'ao-t'ieh* may be seen in Plates 1–8, 22, 23, 28, and 29.

The cicada is also frequently depicted on the bronzes, apparently as a symbol of resurrection. As the cicada, after its larval stage underground, emerges and begins its shrill singing, so it was hoped that the spirits of the dead would once more emerge from the grave and return to life. Designs of eyes often appear in isolation, apparently with magical connotations, and the areas between these larger designs of t'ao-t'ieh, cicadas, and so on, are filled with spiral patterns which are traditionally said to represent clouds or thunder. Occasionally the whole vessel is made in the form of some beast or bird, particularly the owl, which, as a bird of the night, was regarded as the guardian of darkness and hence of the world of the dead (Plate 33). In other cases, only the lid is made in the shape of a beast, as may be seen in the vessel with an elephant-shaped lid pictured in Plates 16–18. Elephants were well known to the Shang people, although whether they were native to North China at this time or were brought from the south is not certain.

In addition to such artistic motifs, the sacrificial vessels often bear the name of the parent or ancestor to whom they were dedicated, or the clan seal of the maker. When the vessels were completed, they were consecrated by being smeared with the blood of a sacrificial animal. The famous passage in *Mencius* (1A. 8) concerning an ox which was being led to slaughter for the consecration of a bell, is a late reflection of this ancient custom.

The sacrificial vessels were designed to be ranged on an altar table, and most of them are accordingly only about 7 to 12 inches in height, though occasionally vessels of a larger size were made. Literary sources mention nine great *ting*, or tripods, that were supposed to have been cast in the time of Yü, the founder of the Hsia Dynasty, and in 1946 just such a large tripod was discovered at the An-yang site. Bearing the inscription "for the worship of our mother Wu," it measures $45\frac{1}{2}$ inches in height, with a width of $42\frac{1}{2}$ inches, and weighs 1929 pounds. It is preserved in the Nanking Museum.

The Shang Dynasty was in time overthrown by the Chou—1027 B.C. is the most generally accepted date. The home of the Chou people was far to the west of An-yang, in the Wei River Valley; their capital, Hao, was situated near present-day

Sian in Shensi. With the fall of An-yang, the Shang craftsmen were undoubtedly taken prisoner and transported to the Chou capital, where they were put to work producing bronzes and other works for the new dynasty. But the Chou Dynasty doled out most of the areas under its control as fiefs to the members of the ruling family, to the chiefs of other clans who had assisted in the overthrow of the Shang Dynasty, or to descendants of former dynasties, and in time the Chou kings lost the power to impose their will upon these vassal rulers. While the feudal states of the eastern and central regions flourished and grew in power, the Chou royal house, with its domain far to the west, gradually declined, and in 770 B.C. barbarian invaders forced the Chou king to move his capital east to the city of Lo, near the present city of Lo-yang. This event marks the close of the period known as Western Chou.

The bronzes of the Western Chou period are marked by a decline in the level of workmanship and an increase in the length of inscriptions. It became customary to cast bronzes to serve not only as offerings to the ancestors but as family treasures to be handed down to one's posterity in commemoration of some important event. The inscriptions ordinarily describe the military or civil achievements of the owner, list the gifts and boons received from the king in recognition of these achievements, and, after appropriate praises of the king's virtues, exhort the owner's heirs to treasure the vessel for generations to come. Sometimes vessels were cast to commemorate the marriage of the daughter of a feudal lord. In other words, the bronzes became less articles for the worship and delight of the spirits than family heirlooms that served to recall the history and merits of one's forebears, a change which reflects the growing humanism of the time.

The earliest musical instruments were probably made of wood or bamboo, but by Shang times the so-called ch'ing, or musical stones, were in use. Oblong in shape and arched in the middle, they were of various sizes and were suspended from a rack, producing a musical scale when struck. With the appearance of bronze, small metal bells were made, and by Chou times, much larger bronze bells were being produced to use in conjunction with the musical stones (Plates 38 and 39). These bells became especially numerous in late Chou times, after the move of the capital to Lo-yang. In addition, the Shang and Chou people used bronze to fashion horse and carriage fittings.

In Shang and early Chou times, the unit of value seems to have been the cowrie shell, and bronze inscriptions often mention strings of cowrie shells that were presented as gifts by the king to his vassals. For this reason, many characters dealing with monetary value, such as those for "buy," "sell," "expensive," "cheap," "wealth," "treasure," and so on, contain the character for cowrie shell in their make-up. Cowrie shells, however, appear to have been too valuable to serve as currency for everyday transactions. In late Chou times, as cities grew in size and trade became increasingly important, a true currency appeared in the form of bronze coins. The earliest bronze coins, which date from around the fourth century B.C., were quite large and were cast in the shape of two common implements, spades and knives, with round or square holes in the handles. In time, these coins were reduced in size, and finally they were replaced almost entirely by round coins. The round coins, however, retained the round or square holes of the old currency, which allowed the user to string them into units of a fixed number.

In late Chou times, during the so-called Warring States period (403–221 B.C.), there was a marked change in the style of decoration used on the bronze vessels produced for sacrificial and household use. The designs became more delicate, and the inscriptions were done in a fine, elongated, and highly decorated style. Whereas the bronzes of the Shang, early Chou, and middle Chou periods had been ornamented with isolated figures of dragons or phoenixes executed in a carefully balanced and symmetrical style, the late Chou pieces are often covered with a single over-all pattern made up of the intricately laced bodies of beasts or serpents (Plates 30 and 31). The appearance of such a pattern is probably related to the popularity at this period of the *yin-yang* philosophy, which attributes all change in the natural world to the interaction of two primal forces, the male or positive force, known as *yang*, and the female or negative force, known as *yin*.

During the Warring States period, the technique of inlaying bronze with gold or silver was developed. The earliest pieces of this type, swords or dagger-axes inlaid with gold, come from the site of the states of Wu, Yüeh, and Ch'u, in the lower Yangtze Valley, and appear to date from early in the Warring States period. No pieces of such an early date have been found in the north, though in time the technique was transmitted to the area of Lo-yang, the center of traditional Chinese culture, and many beautiful inlaid vases, buckles, and other pieces of the late Warring States period have been found there (Colorplate 2 and Plates 40–43).

Metallurgical techniques also progressed during this period. The *Chou Li*, or *Rites of Chou*, a work generally believed to date largely from this period, in the section on technology,[9] gives the following table for the proportions of copper to tin to be used in making various types of bronze objects:

5 parts copper to 1 part tin for bells and tripods

4 parts copper to 1 part tin for axes

3 parts copper to 1 part tin for dagger-axes and halberd heads

2 or 3 parts copper to 1 part tin for large knives

3 parts copper to 2 parts tin for small knives and arrowheads

Equal parts of copper and tin for mirrors and speculums

Chemical analysis reveals that these proportions were not always exactly observed in actual practice; they represent, rather, the general proportions to be followed in order to obtain the degrees of hardness needed for particular categories of objects.

Bronzes of the Shang, early Chou, and middle Chou periods were produced by means of sectional clay moulds, actual fragments of which have been recovered from early sites. But the delicacy of the designs found on late Chou pieces, such as the mir-

[9] "Winter Officials."

rors of the Warring States period, suggests that by this time the lost-wax process was being used. The mirrors show particularly well the fondness for minute and intricate design which is characteristic of this period (Plates 34 and 35). Bronze seals also make their appearance at this time.

During late Chou times, bronze vessels decorated with bands depicting realistic hunting scenes begin to appear, and this tendency continued during the succeeding Ch'in and Han periods. Han-period jars and bowls were often decorated with mountain landscapes inhabited by bears, monkeys, tigers, and various fabulous beasts and immortals, all done in realistic style. During the Han period, perfumed woods were imported from the south, and we find incense burners of various shapes, such as that shown in Plates 36 and 37, as well as lamps in the form of birds or animals. The more traditional types of vessels produced in this period, such as sacrificial tripods or wine vessels, are usually undecorated, or marked with a simple filament known as *hsien-wen*, or string pattern.

JADES

THE SHANG DYNASTY produced not only superb bronzes but extremely fine jade carvings as well. The character for jade was originally the same as the present-day character for "king," i.e., 王, a picture of three pieces of jade threaded on a cord. Later a dot was added to make it readily distinguishable from the character for "king," resulting in the present character for "jade," 玉.

It is not certain where the jade used during the Shang Dynasty came from, though undoubtedly articles, including semiprecious stones, were brought to the Shang court from many regions. From late Neolithic times the Chinese had sought pieces of attractive and high-quality stone to use for axes and personal ornaments, and they probably became acquainted with jade at this time.

The Shang people produced beautiful jade axes and daggers, fitted with ornamented handles made of bronze and inlaid with turquoise. These jade axes and daggers, because of the brittle nature of their blades, do not seem to have been intended for actual use, but were, rather, ceremonial objects designed to enhance the dignity and splendor of the ruler and his nobles. Typical of purely ritual objects of jade is the *ts'ung*, which has square sides and a round depression in the middle, resembling in shape a well or an axle. Its use is uncertain, though the *Rites of Chou* identifies it as an object used in sacrifices to the earth. The shape was imitated in pottery of the Sung period and, later, in the flower vases known as *suan-mu-shou*, in celadon.

In contrast to the *ts'ung* is the type of jade disc known as *pi*, which was associated with the worship of Heaven. The *pi* were also made from large pieces of jade. Most of the specimens we have today date from late Chou or Han times. Since the worship of Heaven was confined to the emperor, it is possible that very few *pi* were made in early times, and this may account for their rarity. Possibly the *pi* only came into existence as a result of the Chou philosophical convention of referring to the earth as round. By late Chou times, however, the *pi* were made in great numbers and were no longer confined to ritual use, but were exchanged as gifts by the feudal lords and were prized as family treasures. It is not clear what the original form of the *pi* was, though it may have derived from the spindle weights used in weaving, grown larger in size as the object shed its original function and became a religious symbol.

The *pi* is characterized by a hole in the center of the disc. According to the *Erh Ya*, a late Chou period collection of glosses on words in the classics, there are actually three different types of jade discs, distinguished by name according to the proportion of the size of the disc to that of the hole in the center. That in which the diameter of the disc is twice the diameter of the hole is known as *huan*; that in which the diameter is three times the diameter of the hole is called *yüan*; and that in which the diameter of the disc is four times the diameter of the whole is called *pi*. The three types may be seen at the top left, top right, and bottom, respectively, of Plate 47. Still another type of jade disc, called a *hsüan-chi*, was an astronomical instrument used, it would seem, for sighting the stars

41

and determining the true celestial pole.

The Shang people also used jade to make ornamental pendants which they hung from their belts. Necklaces were perhaps the most common personal ornaments among ancient peoples, but since the Shang robe was folded together in the front like a kimono, it was unsuited to the wearing of necklaces. The sleeves of the robe were long, which may account for the scarcity of bracelets and rings that have been recovered from Shang sites. In place of such conventional types of jewelry, the Shang people wore pendants, as we have said, or jade decorations on their hats. The existence of this custom in Shang times was unknown until recent excavations brought to light the actual jades, beautifully carved pieces of miniature sculpture representing birds, beasts, or fish (Plates 44 and 45). Among birds, phoenixes are the most commonly depicted, although water birds are also found. In addition to the pendants, there are small hat decorations of jade, and small tubular carvings in the shape of beasts, the use of which is not known.

Poems and other writings of the Chou period contain frequent mentions of jade. In the *Book of Odes*, for example, jade is used as a simile for a lovely young girl[10] and mentioned as the material from which ritual vessels were sometimes made.[11] Similarly, the *Analects*[12] records the remark of Confucius: "Ritual, ritual, they say. Are jades and silks all that is meant by ritual?" From this it is evident that jade played an important part in the material trappings of sacrifices and other rituals of the time. In addition, the jade pendants, which continued to be worn in Chou times, were said to be a constant reminder to the wearer to move in a dignified and decorous manner since they clinked when one moved too rapidly or abruptly.

The symbolic significance which jade had for the ancient Chinese may be appreciated from the following passage recorded in the *Book of Ritual*.[13] Confucius, asked by one of his disciples why jade is valued so highly, replies: "In ancient times, gentle-men compared jade to virtue. Its warm, smooth glossiness is symbolic of benevolence. Its close texture and durability are symbolic of wisdom. It can be angular without breaking, which is symbolic of righteousness. It dangles down as though it had fallen, which is symbolic of propriety . . . . It is only right that the whole world should honor it. Hence the ode ["Airs of Ch'in," "War Chariot"] says:

> *I think of the gentleman,*
> *His warmth is like jade.*

The *Rites of Chou* describes the treasury where the royal jades were kept[14], the duties of the official who had charge of jade objects at court,[15] and those of the craftsmen who carved jade.[16] Such a large part did jade play in the life and language of the time that it eventually became identified with the human body, and the word "jade" was prefixed to nouns referring to parts of the body or personal objects as a kind of honorific, as may be seen in the passage in the *Kuo Yü* (Conversations from the States[17]), . . . "The Great King in person hastened his jade feet."

As a result of the important role of jade in ancient Chinese life, words pertaining to jade articles and varieties of jade became extremely numerous. The earliest Chinese dictionary, the *Shuo-wen Chieh-tzu*, compiled by Hsü Shen, (Preface dated A.D. 100) contains 130 such words, though already by Hsü Shen's time the meaning of many of them was obscure and the exact uses of the various jade articles could in some cases no longer be determined. The fact that the characters for such common expressions as "toy," "to play with," and "rare" contain the element indicating jade shows how fond the Chinese were of the stone.

As we have already noted above in the discussion of bronze, arts and crafts underwent a marked revival during the Warring States period, and workmanship reached a level of skill and delicacy unknown in earlier Chou times. The finest work of this period is represented by the bronzes and jades excavated at the village of Chin-ts'un in the

---

[10] "Airs of Shao-nan," "Dead Deer in the Field."
[11] "Greater Odes," "The Foot of Mt. Han."
[12] XVII. 11.
[13] XLVIII.
[14] "Heavenly Offices," Jade Treasure.
[15] "Spring Officials," Keeper of the Jade Tablet.
[16] "Winter Officials," The Jade Carver.
[17] Wu-yü section.

suburbs of the city of Lo-yang in Honan. The Chou Dynasty, as already mentioned, moved its capital to Lo-yang in 770 B.C. During the centuries that followed, the power of the Chou king declined markedly, though he remained a figure of religious and ritual importance and was still nominal sovereign of the empire. His vassals, the rulers of the numerous feudal states, fought incessantly among themselves, the more powerful of them invading and annexing the territories of their weaker neighbors, until by the period of the Warring States the number had been reduced, for all practical purposes, to seven. The personal domain of the Chou ruler dwindled in size as his political power faded, until he controlled only the immediate area of the capital, and in 256 B.C. even this was taken from him by the ruler of the state of Ch'in; he remained nominal ruler until 249 B.C., when the dynasty finally came to an end.

Although the Chou capital of Lo-yang ceased to be the seat of political power, it remained the center for traditional arts and crafts. The bronzes and jades recovered from Chin-ts'un at Lo-yang show a level of craftsmanship unparalleled by pieces produced during the same period in other areas of China, reminding us that the centers of political power and of artistic activity do not always coincide.

During the Warring States period, the jade discs known as *pi* began to be made in much larger sizes and to be prized as treasures. Works of this period often mention the famous "Jade Disc of Mr. Ho," a treasure of the ruler of the state of Chao, for which the ruler of Ch'in is said to have offered fifteen cities. Some of the *pi* of this period have plain polished surfaces, but most of them are decorated with patterns of the so-called "grain" or "rush mat" varieties. The former consists of a series of small curlicue protuberances resembling seeds of grain (Plates 41 and 47). The latter is a design of interlaced lines, like the pattern of a woven rush mat.

In addition to the jade discs, there were various ceremonial batons, known as *kuei*, *chang*, or *hu*, which derived their shape from the stone axes and knives of the Neolithic period. Made originally of ordinary stone, they were later executed in jade, and still later in ivory or wood. Such batons are still used in ceremonies by Japanese Shinto priests, and are known in Japanese as *shaku*. During the Chou period, they appear to have been bestowed as gifts by a Chou ruler upon his vassals at the enfeoffment ceremony, much as swords were presented to newly enfeoffed vassals in a later period. Originally, the gifts were probably real weapons, which in time altered in shape, becoming merely ritual symbols. Examples of *hu* and *chang* dating from Shang or Chou times may be seen in Plate 46.

The jade pendants of the early period were customarily carved in the shapes of birds, tigers, hares, or fish (Plate 48), as already mentioned. In later times, these gave way to dragons, phoenixes, and other mythical creatures with auspicious connotations. The jades, which formed the principal ornaments, were hung from cords strung with various other smaller decorative stones, though the exact nature of these stones was unknown until recent excavations brought the actual objects to light. We now know that, in addition to the jades, various colored ornaments of agate, amber, crystal, turquoise, malachite, pearl, and glass were used. In addition to pendants, jade was used for hat ornaments, hairpins and the cicada-shaped ceremonial objects called *han*, which were placed in the mouths of corpses before burial, and those shaped like pigs and called *wo*, which were placed in the closed fists of corpses. Jade was also used for ornaments or sword hilts and scabbards, for sash buckles, and for seals.

Various jade-producing areas are mentioned in early texts, such as the region of Lan-t'ien in Shensi; however, the exact locations of these sites is not known today. The most important area was the region of Khotan beyond the western frontier of China. The mountain and river valleys of the Kunlun, Nanshan, and other ranges of this area, particularly of the river known as Yü-lung-ho, or Jade Dragon River, yielded jade of a very high quality. The jades of the Kunlun Mountains were already known by Warring States times, and in the reign of Emperor Wu (140–87 B.C.) of the Han

43

Dynasty, when the region was brought under Chinese control, they were imported to China in large quantities. Han period documents, written on wooden tablets and recovered in recent years from sites in the northwest, indicate that jades were often exchanged as gifts. The custom of referring to old jades in Chinese as *Han-yü*, "Han jades," arose from the fact that so many jade objects dating from the Han period have been found.

Among these early jades, those of a milk-white or green color are most common, though pieces with a pale-yellow or reddish-brown color are also found. Some are even of a very dark hue close to black, but these seem to have come from a different region than did the other types. All are semitranslucent and have a beautiful luster that, unlike the bright, cold shine of crystal, conveys a feeling of inner warmth and stillness. It is for this reason that the Chinese have for so long loved and prized jade and regarded it as a symbol of the human ideal.

The ancient Chinese had learned how to cut and polish stone long before the beginning of the historical era, so that the carving of jade presented no particular technical difficulties to them. But because of its extreme hardness, it was necessary to find an even harder substance with which to polish it. They solved this problem by using garnet dust or corundum, which they mixed with water and applied to saws or awl-like instruments. By drilling or filing for a long period with such instruments and abrasives, they were able to cut the jade, drill holes in it, and work it to the desired shape, after which they polished it with leather and more abrasive. The process of jade working, however, is a very long and slow one that requires almost unending days of effort. Hence the phrase *ch'ieh ts'o cho-mo* (literally, cutting and polishing), taken from bone- and jade-working, came to be used to describe diligent and unremitting effort. It is first found in the *Book of Odes*, in the first song of the "Airs of Wei," and is quoted in the *Analects*, (I. 15), whence it has passed into popular speech.

The particular variety of jade known as jadeite comes from the Kachin Mountains of northern Burma. It may not have been imported to China in ancient times, since no piece dating from the early period has yet been found, but during the eighteenth century, particularly in the reign of the Ch'ing Dynasty Emperor Ch'ien-lung (1738–95), such large quantities of high-quality jadeite were brought to China that many people mistakenly believe the stone to be native to China. During the same period rubies and sapphires were imported from India, and these were combined with the jadeite in the creation of gorgeous necklaces, hat decorations, and other types of jewelry for the rulers and members of the aristocracy. While jadeite of the finest quality, characterized by a pure green color and beautiful luster, was used for such personal ornaments, that of the next best quality, white with streaks of green, was used for articles such as incense burners. Nearly all the present-day rings and sash clips made of high-quality jadeite were actually recarved from the jade jewelry of Ch'ing times.

During the Ch'ing period, parts of Central Asia once more came under Chinese control, and as a result large quantities of jade from the Kunlun Mountains were then imported to China, where the jade craftsmen of Peking, Suchow, and other urban centers carved and finished it. That few jade articles were produced in China during the almost two thousand years between the early Han and the Ch'ing Dynasties is partly due to the fact that the Chinese during this time seldom had control of the jade-producing area of Central Asia. During the period of disunion that followed the breakup of the Han and Chin dynasties, while the north and west were controlled by alien dynasties, the native Chinese rulers were confined mainly to the region of the Yangtze Valley, which lacks jade resources. And although the T'ang Dynasty succeeded in unifying the empire and extending Chinese influence into Central Asia, the men of the T'ang period were far more interested in importing fine horses from the west than in importing jade, and the same may be said of the men of the Sung, Yüan, and Ming dynasties.

Part Three: Commentaries on the Plates

COLORPLATES

1 Jade pendants in the shape of beast and fish. Yellow jade with "grain" pattern; Warring States period; beast 4 1/8 inches, fish 3 1/2 inches. Recovered from the Chin-ts'un site outside the city of Lo-yang, Honan. Collection Hosokawa Goryu.

2 Large vessel with gold, silver, and glass inlay. Warring States period, height 20 inches. An example of the finest workmanship of late Chou times, probably a family treasure of one of the kings or feudal rulers of the time, recovered from the Chin-ts'un site. Collection Hosokawa Goryu.

3 Detail of bail-handled wine vessel (shown in Plate 1).

BLACK–AND–WHITE PLATES

1 Bail-handled wine vessel (*yu*) with *t'ao-t'ieh* design. Shang Dynasty, height 15 1/2 inches. Hakutsuru Art Museum, Kobe.

2-4 Details of a wine vessel (*ho*) with *t'ao-t'ieh* design. Shang Dynasty, height 28 inches. (See Plate 32 for a general view of a wine vessel of the type called *ho*.) This particular *ho* is unusually large. It was recovered from one of the royal tombs of the Shang capital site at An-yang. Plate 4 is a detail of the spout of the vessel. Nezu Art Museum, Tokyo.

5 Detail of the handle of a wine vessel (*chia*) with *t'ao-t'ieh* design. Shang Dynasty, height 28 inches. Recovered from the same site as the piece above. Nezu Art Museum, Tokyo.

6 Bail-handled wine vessel (*yu*) with *t'ao-t'ieh* design, detail of lid. Shang Dynasty, height 12 5/8 inches.

7 Bail-handled wine vessel (*yu*) with *t'ao-t'ieh* design. Shang Dynasty, height 11 7/8 inches. Though closely resembling the vessel shown in detail in Plate 6, this is actually another piece.

8 Drinking cup (*chüeh*) with *t'ao-t'ieh* design. Shang Dynasty, height 8 3/8 inches. Nezu Art Museum, Tokyo.

9 Drinking cups of the types called *chüeh* (left) and *ku* (right). Shang Dynasty. The *chüeh* is 8 inches in height; the *ku* is 11 1/2 inches in height and 6 1/4 inches in diameter at the mouth.

10–12 Square bail-handled wine vessel (*yu*) with crested phoenix design. Shang Dynasty, height 8 inches. Hakutsuru Art Museum, Kobe.

13–15. Bail-handled wine vessel (*yu*) with crested phoenix design and heads of sacrificial beasts. Shang Dynasty, height 12 1/2 inches. Hakutsuru Art Museum, Kobe.

16, 17 Details of vessel, Plate 18 (*top*).

18 (*above*) Vessel with elephant-shaped lid. Shang Dynasty, height 11 3/4 inches. This vessel, known as a *kuang*, was designed for pouring wine. The lid, when removed and placed upside down, forms a convenient base for the vessel to rest on. Hakutsuru Art Museum, Kobe.

(*below*) Vessels of the *kuei* type with bird-shaped handles and wave designs. Shang Dynasty; height 5 1/8 inches, diameter of mouth 7 5/8 inches. Nezu Art Museum, Tokyo.

19 Detail of vessel, Plate 18 (*bottom*).

20, 21 Bail-handled wine vessel (*yu*) with ram's-head handle decorations and crested phoenix design. Shang Dynasty, height 12 5/8 inches. Nezu Art Museum, Tokyo.

22, 23 Square wine vessel (*yi*) with *t'ao-t'ieh* design. Shang Dynasty, height 26 inches. Strictly speaking, the *yi* is a vessel for storing wine, though the term is sometimes used for bronze vessels in general. Judging from the character with which the word is written, it originally indicated the offering of a fowl in sacrifice. Nezu Art Museum, Tokyo.

24, 25 Drinking cup (*chüeh*) with bird-shaped lid and thunder pattern. Chou Dynasty, height 9 1/2 inches. A piece of very unusual shape. Hakutsuru Art Museum, Kobe.

26, 27 Wine vessel (*tsun*) with elephant design. Shang Dynasty, height 11 3/4 inches. The *tsun*, like the *yi*, was a vessel for storing wine. Hakutsuru Art Museum, Kobe.

28, 29 Square wine vessel (*tsun*) with *t'ao-t'ieh* design.

45

Shang Dynasty, height 10 7/8 inches. The decoration on the vessel is divided into four bands. The topmost bears a feather design of long, curving indentations, a design also found on bone hairpins of the period. The second band bears a design of crested phoenixes, the third a *t'ao-t'ieh* design, and the fourth a design of crested dragons.

30, 31 Wine vessel (*tsun*) with a design of coiled dragons. Chou Dynasty; height 12 7/8 inches, diameter of mouth 6 7/8 inches. This type of design, consisting of coiled serpent-like forms, became popular from middle Chou times on. The inscription on the rim gives the name of the owner of the vessel and bids his sons and grandsons treasure and use it forever. Nezu Art Museum, Tokyo.

32 Wine vessel (*ho*). This vessel was excavated at an early date and therefore has a shiny surface. In former times, collectors disliked bronzes with a patina and took care to prevent its formation, but in more recent times patinated bronzes have come to be preferred. The inscription contains a character representing a man making an offering of a child, and the piece is therefore presumed to date from the Shang Dynasty, when children were sometimes used as sacrifices. Height 8 3/4 inches. Nezu Art Museum, Tokyo.

33 Bail-handled wine vessel (*yu*) in the shape of an owl. Shang Dynasty, height 9 1/4 inches. Hakutsuru Art Museum, Kobe.

34, 35 Vessel with cicada design belonging to the Baron of Jui. Chou Dynasty, height 16 inches. The piece contains an inscription indicating that it was made at the request of the Baron. Jui was a small state in the region north of the place where the Yellow River turned east toward the sea. It is often mentioned in the *Book of Odes* and other early texts, and seems, in spite of its small size, to have held a high position among the feudal states of the time. Hosokawa Goryu Collection.

36, 37 Gold-plated incense burner. Han Dynasty, height 5 5/8 inches. The rim bears a long inscription indicating that the piece was made for official use, and contains a date equivalent to 61 B.C. The design on the lid represents three tigers. Tigers and bears are often depicted on Han works, especially on pieces such as this, which are intended for everyday use. Nezu Art Museum, Tokyo.

38, 39 Bell. Warring States period; height 7 1/2 inches, width 5 1/8 inches. Bells were cast in various sizes and were designed to be assembled in sets, one set consisting of sixteen bells. Very few complete sets have been found. Most of the extant examples of bells date from middle or late Chou times. From the point of view of workmanship, this piece, recovered from the Chin-ts'un site outside Lo-yang, probably represents the finest specimen so far discovered. Even the inside of the bell is decorated with a delicate pattern.

40 Large vessel with gold, silver, and glass inlay. See Colorplate 2.

41 Jade pendants. See Colorplate 1.

42 Sash buckle, detail of Plate 43 (*bottom*).

43 (*above*) Green-jade pigs. Han Dynasty; lengths 4 1/2 inches, heights 1 1/4 inches. These are examples of the so-called *wo*, small pieces of jade placed in the fist of a corpse at the time of burial. These, which have small holes drilled at either end, are made of fine-quality green jade and have a particularly beautiful luster. Collection Hosokawa Goryu.
(*below*) Sash buckle. Warring States period; length 6 1/4 inches, height 1 1/4 inches. Made of yellow jade with "grain" pattern decorations, the piece was recovered from the Chin-ts'un site at Lo-yang. The knob in the middle of the under side fitted into a hole in the sash, while a cord fastened to the other end of the sash looped over the head of the buckle. Collection Hosokawa Goryu.

44 Fish-shaped jade pendants. Shang-Chou period. Fish, because of their fertility, were regarded as good-luck symbols and are often depicted in jade. The pair at the top, made of yellow jade, measure 2 7/8 inches in length. The pendant in the middle at the right, of white jade, is 4 1/4 inches. That at the lower left, of yellow jade, is 4 inches; the small piece at the bottom, of yellow jade, is 3 inches. Tokyo National Museum.

45 Jade pendants in various shapes. Shang-Chou period. Top left, a curved beast in green jade, 1 1/2 inches. Right, an insect in green jade, 2 1/8 inces. The piece in the center, a bird in yellow jade, is 1 3/8 inches wide and 1 1/8 inches long. At the bottom, a fish in white jade, 10 3/8 inches. Tokyo National Museum.

46 Ceremonial jade batons. Shang-Chou period. Both forms derive from stone weapons, though in later times their use was purely ritual. That on the left, a *hu*, which takes its shape from a stone knife, is green jade and is 24 inches long. That on the right, a *chang*, deriving from a stone dagger-ax, is black jade, 10 3/8 inches. Tokyo National Museum.

47 Jade discs. Warring States period. At the top left is a *huan*, made of white jade, 1 1/2 inches in diameter. At the top right is a *yüan*, of yellow jade, 2 1/2 inches in diameter. Tokyo National Museum.

48 Bird-shaped jade pendants. The piece at the top, of yellow jade, is 2 3/4 inches; that in the middle, of white jade, 1 3/8 inches; and that at the bottom, of yellow jade, 4 3/8 inches. Tokyo National Museum.

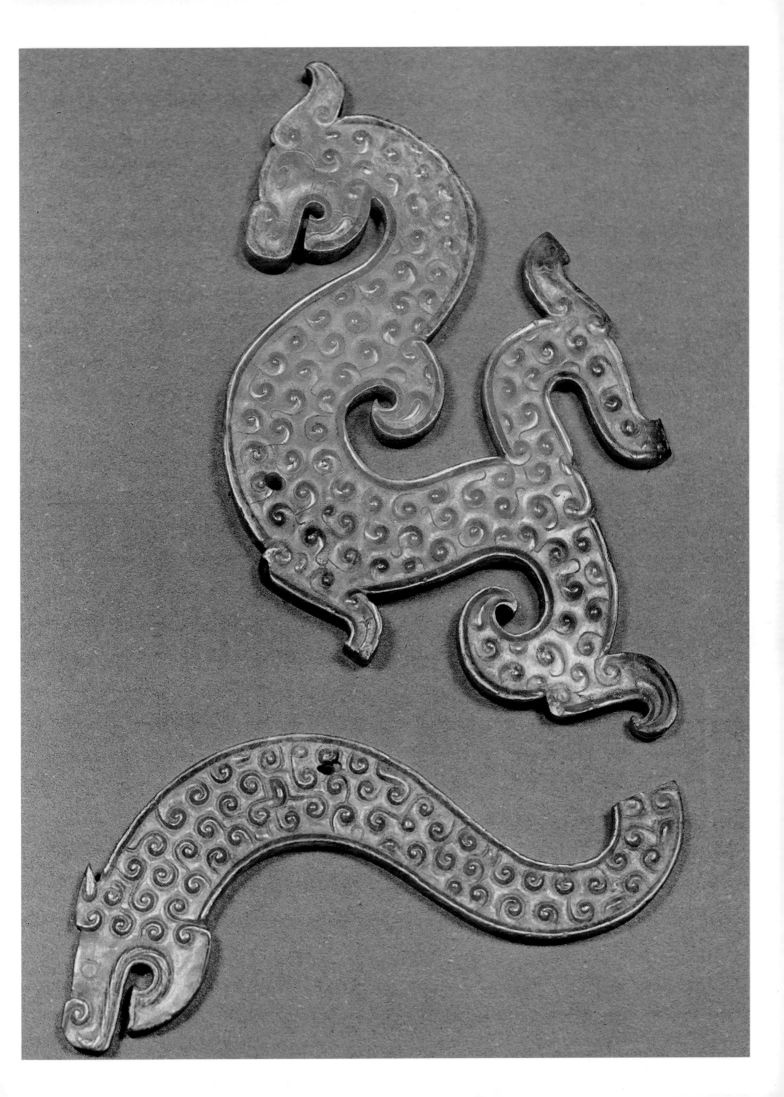

4

7

17

23

24

29

34

35

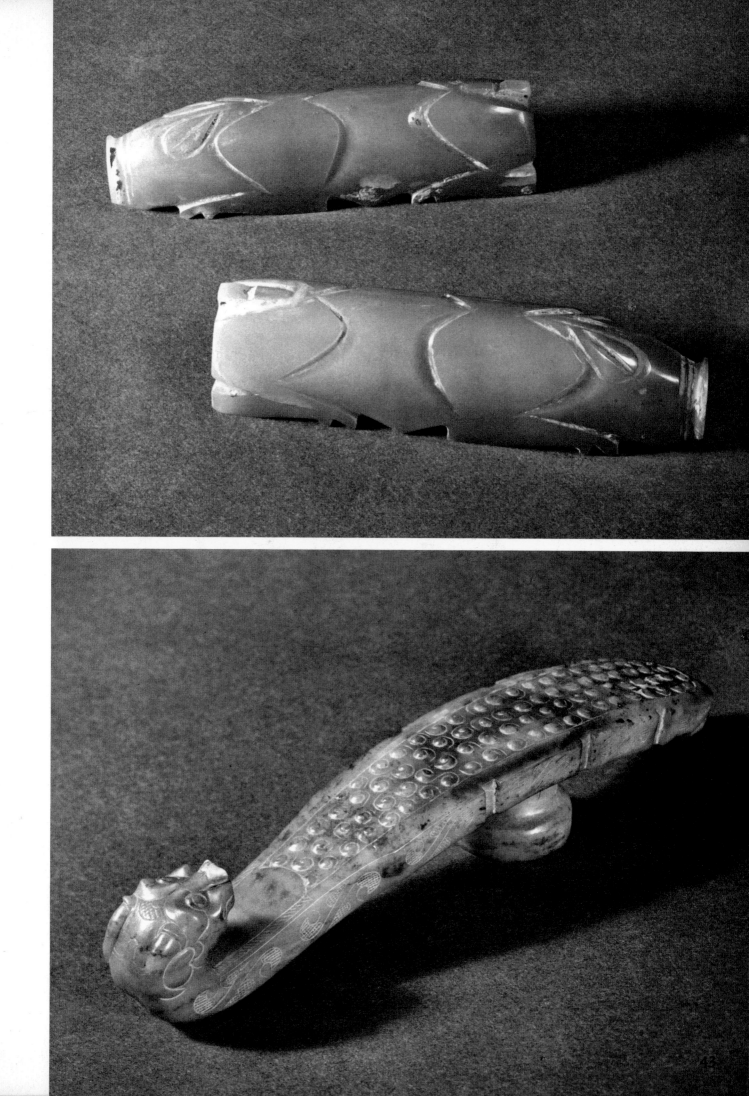